The Ninja Air Fryer Cookbook UK XXL

Effortless & Mouthwatering Dishes for Daily Enjoyment | Global Flavours, Vegan Options, & Full Nutrition Facts | Air Fryer Recipe Book from Breakfast to Dinner

James Churchill

Table of Contents

Introduction 8

  1. How the Ninja Air Fryer Works 8

  2. Essential Tips and Tricks for Perfect Results 10

  3. Must-Have Accessories and Maintenance 11

Chapter 1: Quick Breakfasts for Busy Mornings 15

  Full English Breakfast Wrap 16

  Air Fryer Crumpets with Honey and Butter 17

  Scrambled Egg and Smoked Salmon Croissants 18

  Cheddar and Mushroom Omelette Bites 19

  Toasted Porridge Oat Bars with Sultanas 20

  Air Fryer Breakfast Hash with Sausage and Potatoes ... 21

  Marmite and Cheese Soldiers 22

  Black Pudding and Potato Cakes 23

  Bacon and Tomato Breakfast Muffins 24

  Grilled Kippers with Lemon and Parsley 25

  Breakfast Scones with Bacon and Egg 26

  Spinach and Feta Breakfast Pasties 27

  Cinnamon and Apple Breakfast Rolls 28

  Air Fryer Kedgeree Bites 29

  Avocado and Poached Egg on Toast 30

Chapter 2: Family-Friendly Dinners 31

  Air Fryer Cottage Pie with Crispy Potato Topping 32

  Chicken Tikka Masala with Pilau Rice 33

  Bangers and Mash with Onion Gravy 34

  Roast Beef with Yorkshire Puddings 35

  Shepherd's Pie with a Golden Crust 36

  Lamb Koftas with Mint Yoghurt Dip 37

Crispy Breaded Haddock with Chips 38

Chicken and Mushroom Pie with Puff Pastry 39

Air Fryer Sausage Rolls with Mustard 40

Roast Chicken with Herby Potatoes 41

Beef Wellington Bites 42

Gammon Steaks with Pineapple 43

Toad in the Hole with Gravy 44

Fish Finger Butties with Tartare Sauce 45

Steak and Kidney Pudding 46

Chicken and Leek Hotpot 47

Pork Belly Bites with Apple Sauce 48

Beef and Ale Pie with Crispy Pastry 49

Battered Cod with Chunky Chips 50

Cornish Pasties with Steak Filling 51

Chapter 3: Light and Healthy Lunches 53

Grilled Halloumi and Aubergine Salad 54

Air Fryer Jacket Potatoes with Cottage Cheese 55

Roast Veggie Wrap with Hummus 56

Prawn and Avocado Salad with Lemon Dressing 57

Butternut Squash and Quinoa Salad 58

Air Fryer Falafel Wraps with Tahini 59

Tuna Nicoise Salad with New Potatoes 60

Grilled Chicken Caesar Wraps 61

Beetroot and Goat's Cheese Salad 62

Smoked Mackerel and Cucumber Salad 63

Roast Veggie and Feta Couscous 64

Poached Salmon and Watercress Sandwiches 65

Air Fryer Chickpea and Sweet Potato Patties 66

Mediterranean Stuffed Peppers 67

Grilled Asparagus and Poached Egg Salad 68

Avocado, Tomato and Mozzarella Salad 69

Air Fryer Lemon and Herb Chicken Skewers 70

Spinach and Ricotta Stuffed Mushrooms 71

Grilled Courgette and Red Pepper Paninis... 72

Pear, Walnut, and Stilton Salad 73

Chapter 4: Fish and Seafood Delights.. 75

Air Fryer Fish and Chips with Mushy Peas 76

Crispy Battered Prawns with Sweet Chilli Dip 77

Grilled Mackerel with Lemon and Thyme.. 78

Smoked Haddock Fishcakes with a Crispy Coating.. 79

Breaded Sole Fillets with Tartar Sauce 80

Air Fryer Scallops with Garlic Butter 81

Grilled Seabass with Herby Potatoes 82

Prawn and Avocado Cocktail with a Twist 83

Air Fryer Calamari with Lemon Aioli 84

Haddock and Leek Fish Pie 85

Air Fryer Salmon with Dill and Lemon 86

Crab Cakes with a Zesty Mayo 87

Grilled Tuna Steaks with a Soy and Ginger Marinade... 88

Crispy Whitebait with a Lemon Wedge 89

Air Fryer Cod with a Herb Crust 90

Grilled Lobster Tails with Garlic Butter 91

Baked Sea Bream with Fennel and Lemon 92

Plaice Goujons with Homemade Chips 93

Prawn and Chorizo Skewers... 94

Air Fryer Monkfish with Garlic and Parsley 95

Chapter 5: Meat-Free Favourites... 97

Stuffed Aubergines with Couscous and Feta 98

Grilled Cauliflower Steaks with Pesto 99

Air Fryer Falafel with Hummus Dip 100

Roasted Butternut Squash with Quinoa and Herbs 101

Air Fryer Halloumi Fries with Sweet Chilli Sauce.. 102

Crispy Tofu Bites with Soy Dip.. 103

Grilled Vegetable Skewers with Halloumi 104

Lentil Shepherd's Pie with Crispy Topping 105

Mushroom and Spinach Wellington 106

Courgette Fritters with Mint Yoghurt 107

Aubergine Parmigiana with a Crunchy Top 108

Chickpea and Spinach Patties with Tahini 109

Crispy Roasted Sweet Potato Wedges 110

Air Fryer Stuffed Peppers with Rice and Vegetables 111

Grilled Portobello Mushrooms with Garlic and Cheese 112

Chapter 6: Sweet Treats and Desserts 113

Air Fryer Victoria Sponge Bites 114

Sticky Toffee Pudding with Caramel Sauce 115

Apple and Cinnamon Turnovers 116

Jam Doughnuts with Raspberry Filling 117

Bakewell Tartlets with Almond Icing 118

Air Fryer Lemon Drizzle Cake Slices 119

Fudge Brownies with a Gooey Centre 120

Scones with Clotted Cream and Jam 121

Pear and Almond Tart 122

Eccles Cakes with Flaky Pastry 123

Rhubarb and Custard Crumble 124

Air Fryer Shortbread Fingers 125

Chocolate Chip Cookies with a Crispy Edge 126

Honeycomb Crunch Bars 127

Mini Banoffee Pies 128

Disclaimer 129

EXCLUSIVE BONUS

40 Weight Loss Recipes

&

14 Days Meal Plan

Scan the QR-Code and receive
the FREE download:

Introduction

1. How the Ninja Air Fryer Works

The Ninja Air Fryer is a game-changer for home cooking, transforming everyday meals with ease and efficiency. At its core, it functions like a powerful fan oven, using rapid air circulation to create that golden, crispy texture on the outside of your food, while keeping it moist and tender inside. This air fryer requires very little oil – often just a light spray – to achieve results that would typically need deep-frying, making it a healthier option without compromising on flavour.

Understanding the Settings:

- ❖ The Ninja Air Fryer offers several settings that go beyond standard air frying:

- ❖ Air Fry: Perfect for achieving crispy chips, roasted vegetables, or even healthier alternatives to fried chicken. This function circulates hot air intensely around the food, cooking it evenly on all sides.

- ❖ Roast: Ideal for cooking larger cuts of meat or vegetables, this setting mimics traditional oven roasting but with faster results. It's excellent for a Sunday roast or creating a rich, caramelised flavour in vegetables.

- ❖ Reheat: Great for leftovers, this setting gently heats your food without drying it out, so you can enjoy dishes like pizza, pasta, or roasted meats as fresh as they were when first cooked.

❖ Dehydrate: Perfect for making dried fruits, jerky, or vegetable crisps, the dehydrate function uses low heat over a longer time, extracting moisture while preserving flavour and nutrients.

Key Benefits:

The Ninja Air Fryer's versatility makes it a powerful addition to any kitchen. Its quick cooking times save you valuable minutes during busy days, and with minimal preheating required, you can dive right into your recipes without the wait. You'll find the Ninja Air Fryer reduces oil consumption significantly, transforming chips, chicken, and baked treats into lighter versions of your favourites – all while maintaining delicious flavour and crunch.

With just a few practice runs, you'll soon be cooking everything from breakfasts to desserts with ease and consistency.

2. Essential Tips and Tricks for Perfect Results

Achieving the best results with your Ninja Air Fryer is all about technique. Here are some essential tips to ensure your dishes turn out crisp, golden, and delicious every time:

1. Don't Overcrowd the Basket

To ensure even cooking and maximise crispiness, always arrange food in a single layer with a bit of space between each piece. Overcrowding reduces airflow and can leave food soggy. If you're cooking larger batches, it's better to cook in multiple rounds for the best results.

2. A Light Spray of Oil

While the air fryer's design requires little to no oil, a light spray on certain foods can enhance their crispiness. Use an oil spray bottle to mist a thin, even layer without overdoing it. Oils with a high smoke point, like rapeseed or olive oil, work particularly well in the Ninja Air Fryer.

3. Shake or Flip Midway

For foods like chips, chicken wings, or roasted vegetables, giving the basket a shake halfway through cooking helps them brown evenly. Alternatively, turn foods over using tongs if they're too delicate to shake. This simple step can make all the difference in achieving that even, golden crust.

4. Preheat When Needed

While the Ninja Air Fryer doesn't always require preheating, doing so can improve results for recipes that need a quick, intense heat. Just a couple of minutes on the desired setting is usually enough to bring it up to temperature and help food cook more evenly.

5. Season After Cooking

To keep herbs, spices, or dry coatings from burning or falling off, consider seasoning or salting your food after it's cooked. This technique is particularly helpful for chips and roasted vegetables, where a final sprinkle of salt or spices adds that extra burst of flavour.

With these tips, you'll be well-equipped to tackle a wide range of recipes in your Ninja Air Fryer, making each dish as tasty and perfectly cooked as possible.

3. Must-Have Accessories and Maintenance

To get the most out of your Ninja Air Fryer, a few handy accessories and maintenance practices can make all the difference. These items and tips not only expand your cooking options but also help keep your air fryer in top condition for years to come.

Essential Accessories:

1. Silicone Baking Mats

These non-stick mats are ideal for preventing food from sticking to the basket and are especially useful when cooking delicate items like fish or pastries. They also make cleaning up much easier and can be reused for countless cooking sessions.

2. Metal Racks

A metal rack is great for cooking on multiple levels, allowing you to cook larger quantities or different items at once. These racks are particularly useful for things like chips or vegetable crisps, as they help maximise airflow and ensure an even, crispy finish.

3. Reusable Liners

Reusable liners protect the base of the air fryer basket, catching crumbs and any excess grease while preventing food from sticking. These liners are easy to clean and can be a practical way to keep your air fryer in excellent condition.

4. Oil Spray Bottle

A refillable oil spray bottle allows you to apply a light, even mist of oil to your food, ensuring just enough oil for crispiness without going overboard. This is especially handy for dishes like chips, which benefit from a light coating of oil for that perfect crunch.

Maintenance Tips:

1. Regular Cleaning

To keep your Ninja Air Fryer in top shape, clean the basket and tray after each use. Avoid using abrasive sponges or harsh chemicals that could damage the non-stick coating. A gentle wipe-down with warm, soapy water works best for daily cleaning.

2. Monthly Deep Clean

Every few weeks, give your air fryer a deeper clean. Remove the basket and tray, soak them in warm soapy water, and scrub gently to remove any built-up grease or residue. Wipe down the interior of the air fryer to prevent any lingering smells or burnt-on bits.

3. Ventilation Check

Ensure that your Ninja Air Fryer's vents are kept clean and free from blockages. A soft brush or cloth can be used to gently remove any dust or debris from the vents, helping to maintain airflow and prevent overheating.

With the right accessories and a bit of care, your Ninja Air Fryer can become an essential tool in the kitchen, delivering delicious results time after time. By keeping it clean and equipped with these handy add-ons, you'll enjoy a smoother cooking experience and consistently impressive dishes, from simple snacks to full family meals.

EXCLUSIVE BONUS

40 Weight Loss Recipes

&

14 Days Meal Plan

Scan the QR-Code and receive
the FREE download:

Chapter 1:
Quick Breakfasts for Busy Mornings

Full English Breakfast Wrap

SERVINGS: 2 | DIFFICULTY: EASY | TEMPERATURE: 180°C
PREPARATION TIME: 15 MINUTES | COOKING TIME: 10 MINUTES

Ingredients:

* 2 large flour tortillas
* 2 eggs
* 2 rashers of bacon
* 2 sausages
* 100g mushrooms, sliced
* 100g cherry tomatoes, halved
* 2 tbsp baked beans
* 50g cheddar cheese, grated
* salt and pepper to taste
* 1 tbsp olive oil

Preparation:

1. Start by preheating your air fryer to 180°C.
2. In a frying pan, heat the olive oil over medium heat and cook the bacon along with the sausages until golden brown.
3. Remove the bacon and sausages from the pan and allow them to cool slightly. Slice the bacon and sausages into bite-sized pieces.
4. In the same pan, sauté the mushrooms until softened and lightly browned.
5. Whisk the eggs in a small bowl and season with salt and pepper. Gently scramble them in a separate clean pan.
6. Lay out the flour tortillas on a flat surface. Evenly distribute the cooked bacon, sausages, scrambled eggs, mushrooms, cherry tomatoes, and baked beans onto each tortilla.
7. Sprinkle grated cheddar cheese over the top of the ingredients in each wrap.
8. Carefully roll each tortilla into a wrap, tucking in the sides as you go.
9. Place the wraps in the preheated air fryer basket, seam side down, and cook for 8-10 minutes until the tortillas are crispy and the cheese has melted.
10. Once cooked, remove from the air fryer, slice in half, and serve immediately.

NUTRITION FACTS PER 100G:
Energy: 210 kcal | Protein: 8g | Total Fat: 13g | Saturated Fat: 4g
Carbohydrates: 15g | Sugars: 2g | Dietary Fibre: 2g

Air Fryer Crumpets with Honey and Butter

SERVINGS: 4 | DIFFICULTY: EASY | TEMPERATURE: 180°C
PREPARATION TIME: 10 MINUTES | COOKING TIME: 15 MINUTES

Ingredients:

* 250g plain flour
* 1 tsp baking powder
* 1 tsp sugar
* 1/2 tsp salt
* 250ml warm milk
* 1 tbsp unsalted butter, melted
* 1 tsp instant yeast
* 2 tbsp honey
* additional butter for spreading

Preparation:

1. Begin by combining the flour, baking powder, sugar, and salt in a large mixing bowl.
2. Gradually whisk in the warm milk until a smooth batter forms.
3. Stir in the melted butter and sprinkle the instant yeast over the top, then mix well.
4. Allow the mixture to rest for 5 minutes until it starts to bubble slightly.
5. Preheat the air fryer to 180°C.
6. Lightly grease silicone crumpet rings and place them in the air fryer basket.
7. Carefully pour the batter into each ring until they're half-filled.
8. Cook in the air fryer for 10 minutes or until the tops are firm and bubbling.
9. Remove the rings and flip the crumpets; cook for an additional 5 minutes.
10. Once done, remove the crumpets and spread each with a generous amount of butter.
11. Drizzle the honey over the warm crumpets just before serving.

NUTRITION FACTS PER 100G:
Energy: 242 kcal | Protein: 6g | Total Fat: 6g | Saturated Fat: 3g
Carbohydrates: 42g | Sugars: 10g | Dietary Fibre: 1g

Scrambled Egg and Smoked Salmon Croissants

SERVINGS: 4 | DIFFICULTY: EASY | TEMPERATURE: 180°C
PREPARATION TIME: 10 MINUTES | COOKING TIME: 8 MINUTES

Ingredients:

* 4 butter croissants
* 6 large eggs
* 80ml double cream
* 100g smoked salmon
* 2 tbsp chopped chives
* 1 tbsp butter
* salt, to taste
* black pepper, to taste

Preparation:

1. Start by slicing each croissant in half horizontally.
2. In a mixing bowl, whisk together eggs, double cream, salt, and black pepper until well combined.
3. Heat a non-stick pan over medium heat and melt the butter.
4. Pour in the egg mixture and gently stir with a spatula, cooking until the eggs are softly scrambled.
5. Incorporate the chopped chives and remove the pan from heat.
6. Place the bottom halves of the croissants in the air fryer basket.
7. Layer each with a portion of scrambled eggs and slices of smoked salmon.
8. Cover with the top halves of the croissants.
9. Air fry the filled croissants at 180°C for 3-4 minutes or until lightly toasted and warm.
10. Finally, serve immediately and enjoy the delicious combination.

NUTRITION FACTS PER 100G:
Energy: 280 kcal | Protein: 9g | Total Fat: 20g | Saturated Fat: 9g
Carbohydrates: 17g | Sugars: 3g | Dietary Fibre: 1g

Cheddar and Mushroom Omelette Bites

SERVINGS: 4 | DIFFICULTY: EASY | TEMPERATURE: 180°C
PREPARATION TIME: 10 MINUTES | COOKING TIME: 12 MINUTES

Ingredients:

* 6 large eggs
* 100g cheddar cheese, grated
* 100g button mushrooms, finely chopped
* 50ml milk
* 1 tbsp olive oil
* salt, to taste
* black pepper, to taste
* 1 tbsp fresh parsley, chopped (optional)

Preparation:

1. Begin by cracking the eggs into a bowl and whisking them together with the milk until well combined.
2. Stir in the grated cheddar cheese and season with salt and black pepper according to your preference.
3. Heat the olive oil in a small frying pan over medium heat and sauté the chopped mushrooms until soft, which should take about 3–4 minutes.
4. Incorporate the sautéed mushrooms into the egg mixture and mix thoroughly.
5. Preheat the air fryer to 180°C for a couple of minutes.
6. Lightly grease silicone muffin moulds or ramekins with some olive oil.
7. Pour the egg mixture evenly into the prepared moulds, allowing a little space for the omelette bites to rise.
8. Arrange the moulds in the air fryer basket carefully.
9. Cook the omelette bites for approximately 12 minutes, or until they are firm and slightly golden on top.
10. Remove from the air fryer and let them cool slightly before removing from the moulds.
11. Garnis with fresh parsley if desired and serve warm.

NUTRITION FACTS PER 100G:
Energy: 160 kcal | Protein: 11g | Total Fat: 12g | Saturated Fat: 4g
Carbohydrates: 2g | Sugars: 1g | Dietary Fibre: 1g

Toasted Porridge Oat Bars with Sultanas

SERVINGS: 12 | DIFFICULTY: EASY | TEMPERATURE: 160°C
PREPARATION TIME: 15 MINUTES | COOKING TIME: 20 MINUTES

Ingredients:

* 250g porridge oats
* 100g sultanas
* 100g honey
* 75g unsalted butter
* 50g light brown sugar
* 1 tsp vanilla extract
* 1/2 tsp ground cinnamon
* pinch of salt

Preparation:

1. Start by setting your air fryer to preheat at 160°C.
2. In a saucepan over low heat, melt the butter along with the honey, light brown sugar, and vanilla extract. Stir continuously until the sugar has completely dissolved.
3. Combine the porridge oats, sultanas, ground cinnamon, and salt in a mixing bowl. Mix well to ensure the ingredients are evenly distributed.
4. Pour the melted mixture from the saucepan over the dry ingredients in the bowl. Stir thoroughly to coat all the oats and sultanas with the liquid mixture.
5. Line a square baking tin with parchment paper. Transfer the oat mixture into the prepared tin, pressing it down evenly with a spatula to ensure a compact, even layer.
6. Carefully place the baking tin into the air fryer basket. Set the air fryer timer for 20 minutes.
7. Once the cooking time is up, remove the tin from the air fryer and allow it to cool completely at room temperature before slicing into bars.
8. Serve the toasted porridge oat bars as a delicious snack or breakfast treat.

NUTRITION FACTS PER 100G:
Energy: 406 kcal | Protein: 5g | Total Fat: 15g | Saturated Fat: 7g
Carbohydrates: 64g | Sugars: 32g | Dietary Fibre: 5g

Air Fryer Breakfast Hash with Sausage and Potatoes

SERVINGS: 4 | DIFFICULTY: EASY | TEMPERATURE: 180°C
PREPARATION TIME: 10 MINUTES | COOKING TIME: 20 MINUTES

Ingredients:

* 200g sausage, sliced
* 300g potatoes, diced
* 1 red bell pepper, diced
* 1 onion, chopped
* 1 tbsp olive oil
* 1 tsp smoked paprika
* 1/2 tsp garlic powder
* salt and pepper, to taste
* fresh parsley, chopped, for garnish

Preparation:

1. Preheat the air fryer to 180°C.
2. In a bowl, combine the diced potatoes, red bell pepper, and onion with olive oil, smoked paprika, garlic powder, salt, and pepper.
3. Toss the sliced sausage into the mixture, ensuring everything is evenly coated.
4. Place the mixture in the air fryer basket, spreading evenly for even cooking.
5. Cook in the air fryer for 20 minutes, shaking the basket halfway through to ensure even crisping.
6. Once done, remove the hash from the air fryer and garnish with fresh parsley before serving.

NUTRITION FACTS PER 100G:
Energy: 130 kcal | Protein: 5g | Total Fat: 8g | Saturated Fat: 3g
Carbohydrates: 10g | Sugars: 2g | Dietary Fibre: 2g

Marmite and Cheese Soldiers

SERVINGS: 2 | DIFFICULTY: EASY | TEMPERATURE: 180°C
PREPARATION TIME: 5 MINUTES | COOKING TIME: 10 MINUTES

Ingredients:

* 4 slices of wholemeal bread
* 2 tbsp Marmite
* 100g grated mature cheddar cheese
* 50g unsalted butter
* 1 tbsp olive oil

Preparation:

1. Begin by spreading the Marmite evenly over two slices of wholemeal bread.
2. Sprinkle half of the grated cheddar cheese over the Marmite layer.
3. Top with the remaining slices of bread to form sandwiches.
4. Thinly spread butter on the outer sides of each sandwich.
5. Preheat the air fryer to 180°C.
6. Lightly brush the air fryer basket with olive oil to prevent sticking.
7. Place the sandwiches in the air fryer basket without overlapping.
8. Air fry for 5 minutes, then turn the sandwiches over.
9. Continue cooking for another 5 minutes or until golden brown and crispy.
10. Once cooked, cut each sandwich into strips to create soldiers. Serve immediately.

NUTRITION FACTS PER 100G:
Energy: 348 kcal | Protein: 14g | Total Fat: 24g | Saturated Fat: 12g
Carbohydrates: 20g | Sugars: 2g | Dietary Fibre: 3g

Black Pudding and Potato Cakes

SERVINGS: 4 | DIFFICULTY: MEDIUM | TEMPERATURE: 200°C
PREPARATION TIME: 15 MINUTES | COOKING TIME: 20 MINUTES

Ingredients:

* 300g potatoes, peeled and cubed
* 150g black pudding, crumbled
* 50g plain flour
* 1 egg, beaten
* 50g breadcrumbs
* 1 tbsp vegetable oil
* salt and pepper, to taste
* optional: fresh parsley, chopped for garnishing

Preparation:

1. Begin by boiling the potatoes in a saucepan of salted water for about 10 minutes or until soft. Drain and allow to cool slightly.
2. Mash the cooled potatoes in a large mixing bowl until smooth.
3. Mix in the crumbled black pudding, stirring until evenly distributed.
4. Add salt and pepper to taste, then shape the mixture into small cakes.
5. Prepare three separate shallow dishes: one with flour, another with the beaten egg, and the last with breadcrumbs.
6. Coat each cake in flour first, then dip in the beaten egg, and finally cover with breadcrumbs.
7. Lightly brush the cakes with vegetable oil.
8. Preheat the air fryer to 200°C.
9. Arrange the cakes in a single layer in the air fryer basket, cooking in batches if necessary.
10. Air fry the cakes for 8-10 minutes on each side or until golden and crisp.
11. Once done, remove from the air fryer and garnish with chopped parsley if desired.

NUTRITION FACTS PER 100G:
Energy: 210 kcal | Protein: 8g | Total Fat: 11g | Saturated Fat: 3g
Carbohydrates: 21g | Sugars: 1g | Dietary Fibre: 2g

Bacon and Tomato Breakfast Muffins

SERVINGS: 4 | DIFFICULTY: EASY | TEMPERATURE: 180°C
PREPARATION TIME: 10 MINUTES | COOKING TIME: 15 MINUTES

Ingredients:

* 4 slices of smoked bacon
* 150g cherry tomatoes, halved
* 4 large eggs
* 50ml milk
* 50g cheddar cheese, grated
* 1 tbsp fresh chives, chopped
* salt and pepper to taste
* cooking oil spray

Preparation:

1. Begin by preheating your air fryer to 180°C.
2. Next, lightly spray the muffin moulds with cooking oil to prevent sticking.
3. Cook the bacon in the air fryer for about 5 minutes until crispy, then remove and crumble into small pieces.
4. In a mixing bowl, whisk together the eggs and milk until well combined.
5. Stir in the grated cheddar cheese, chopped chives, and cooled bacon into the egg mixture. Season with salt and pepper.
6. Divide the cherry tomato halves among the muffin moulds, placing them cut side up.
7. Pour the egg and bacon mixture evenly over the tomatoes in each mould.
8. Carefully place the filled moulds in the air fryer basket.
9. Cook for 10 minutes, or until the muffins are set and golden on top.
10. Allow the muffins to cool slightly before removing from the moulds. Serve warm and enjoy your delightful breakfast treat.

NUTRITION FACTS PER 100G:
Energy: 197 kcal | Protein: 12g | Total Fat: 15g | Saturated Fat: 6g
Carbohydrates: 3g | Sugars: 2g | Dietary Fibre: 1g

Grilled Kippers with Lemon and Parsley

SERVINGS: 2 | DIFFICULTY: EASY | TEMPERATURE: 200°C
PREPARATION TIME: 5 MINUTES | COOKING TIME: 10 MINUTES

Ingredients:

* 2 whole kippers, about 150g each
* 1 tbsp olive oil
* 1 lemon, sliced
* 2 tbsp fresh parsley, chopped
* salt, to taste
* black pepper, to taste

Preparation:

1. Begin by preheating the air fryer to 200°C.
2. In a small bowl, mix the olive oil with a pinch of salt and black pepper.
3. Brush the kippers with the seasoned olive oil mixture, ensuring even coverage.
4. Place the kippers in the air fryer basket, laying the lemon slices on top.
5. Cook the kippers for 8-10 minutes, or until cooked through and slightly crispy on the edges.
6. Once done, carefully remove the kippers from the air fryer and transfer to a serving plate.
7. Garnish liberally with chopped parsley before serving immediately.

NUTRITION FACTS PER 100G:
Energy: 180 kcal | Protein: 18g | Total Fat: 12g | Saturated Fat: 2g
Carbohydrates: 1g | Sugars: 0g | Dietary Fibre: 1g

Breakfast Scones with Bacon and Egg

SERVINGS: 4 | DIFFICULTY: MODERATE | TEMPERATURE: 200°C
PREPARATION TIME: 15 MINUTES | COOKING TIME: 10 MINUTES

Ingredients:

* 200g plain flour
* 1 tbsp baking powder
* 50g unsalted butter, cubed
* 120ml milk
* 1 large egg
* 4 slices streaky bacon
* 50g mature cheddar cheese, grated
* salt and pepper, to taste

Preparation:

1. Begin by preheating the air fryer to 200°C.
2. In a mixing bowl, combine the flour, baking powder, and a pinch of salt.
3. Incorporate the butter into the flour mixture using your fingertips until it resembles breadcrumbs.
4. Pour in the milk gradually, stirring until a soft dough forms.
5. Roll out the dough on a floured surface until it is about 5cm thick, then cut into 4 scones.
6. Crack the egg into a small bowl, season with salt and pepper, and beat lightly.
7. Brush the top of each scone with the beaten egg, ensuring an even coat.
8. Lay the bacon slices in the air fryer basket and cook for 5 minutes until crispy. Remove and set aside.
9. Place the scones in the air fryer and cook for 10 minutes.
10. After 5 minutes, sprinkle cheese on top of each scone and place a piece of bacon on each before continuing to cook.
11. Once the cheese has melted and the scones are golden, remove them from the air fryer.
12. Serve the breakfast scones warm.

NUTRITION FACTS PER 100G:
Energy: 280 kcal | Protein: 10g | Total Fat: 15g | Saturated Fat: 8g
Carbohydrates: 27g | Sugars: 2g | Dietary Fibre: 1g

Spinach and Feta Breakfast Pasties

SERVINGS: 4 | DIFFICULTY: EASY | TEMPERATURE: 180°C
PREPARATION TIME: 20 MINUTES | COOKING TIME: 15 MINUTES

Ingredients:

* 200g fresh spinach
* 150g feta cheese, crumbled
* 1 tbsp olive oil
* 1 small onion, finely chopped
* 1 clove garlic, minced
* 2 sheets ready-rolled puff pastry
* 1 egg, beaten
* salt and black pepper to taste

Preparation:

1. Begin by heating the olive oil in a pan over medium heat. Add the chopped onion and cook until softened.
2. Stir in the garlic and sauté for another minute. Toss in the fresh spinach and cook until wilted, then remove from heat and let it cool slightly.
3. In a mixing bowl, combine the cooked spinach mixture with crumbled feta cheese. Season with salt and black pepper.
4. Unroll the ready-rolled puff pastry sheets and cut each into 4 equal squares.
5. Spoon a portion of the spinach and feta mixture onto one half of each pastry square, leaving a border around the edges.
6. Brush the edges of the pastry with the beaten egg, then fold the other half over the filling to form a triangle. Press the edges with a fork to seal.
7. Lightly brush the tops of the pasties with the remaining beaten egg.
8. Arrange the pasties in the air fryer basket in a single layer, making sure not to overcrowd.
9. Air fry at 180°C for about 12-15 minutes, or until the pastry is golden and crisp.
10. Once cooked, let the pasties cool slightly before serving.

NUTRITION FACTS PER 100G:
Energy: 270 kcal | Protein: 6g | Total Fat: 20g | Saturated Fat: 8g
Carbohydrates: 16g | Sugars: 1g | Dietary Fibre: 1g

Cinnamon and Apple Breakfast Rolls

SERVINGS: 8 | DIFFICULTY: MEDIUM | TEMPERATURE: 180°C
PREPARATION TIME: 20 MINUTES | COOKING TIME: 12 MINUTES

Ingredients:

* 250g plain flour
* 7g sachet fast-action yeast
* 50g caster sugar
* 125ml warm milk
* 1 egg
* 25g unsalted butter, melted

* 1 tsp ground cinnamon
* 2 small apples, peeled, cored, and diced
* 50g light brown sugar
* 1 tsp vanilla extract
* 1 tbsp vegetable oil for brushing

Preparation:

1. Begin by combining the plain flour, yeast, and caster sugar in a large bowl.
2. In a separate jug, whisk together the warm milk, egg, and melted butter.
3. Pour the wet ingredients into the dry mixture, stirring until a dough forms.
4. Turn the dough onto a floured surface and knead for about 5 minutes until smooth and elastic.
5. Place the dough back into the bowl, cover with a tea towel, and let it rise in a warm spot for about 45 minutes, or until doubled in size.
6. While the dough is rising, prepare the filling by mixing the ground cinnamon, diced apples, light brown sugar, and vanilla extract in a small bowl.
7. Once the dough has risen, roll it out on a floured surface into a rectangle about 1cm thick.
8. Spread the apple-cinnamon mixture evenly over the dough.
9. Roll the dough tightly from one long side to the other, forming a log.
10. Cut the log into 8 even slices.
11. Lightly brush the air fryer basket with vegetable oil.
12. Arrange the rolls in the air fryer basket, ensuring they're not overcrowded.
13. Set the air fryer to 180°C and cook for 12 minutes, or until golden brown and cooked through.
14. Allow to cool slightly before serving warm.

NUTRITION FACTS PER 100G:
Energy: 230 kcal | Protein: 4g | Total Fat: 5g | Saturated Fat: 2g
Carbohydrates: 42g | Sugars: 15g | Dietary Fibre: 2g

Air Fryer Kedgeree Bites

SERVINGS: 4 | DIFFICULTY: MEDIUM | TEMPERATURE: 190°C
PREPARATION TIME: 20 MINUTES | COOKING TIME: 15 MINUTES

Ingredients:

* 150g basmati rice
* 200g smoked haddock, skin removed
* 2 large eggs
* 50g butter
* 1 onion, finely chopped
* 1 tsp mild curry powder
* 2 tbsp fresh parsley, chopped
* 1 tbsp fresh coriander, chopped
* 1 lemon, zested and juiced
* 100g plain flour
* salt and pepper, to taste
* 75g breadcrumbs

Preparation:

1. Begin by cooking the basmati rice according to the packet instructions. Set aside to cool.
2. In a small saucepan, place the smoked haddock and enough water to cover. Simmer for about 5 minutes until cooked through. Drain, flake the fish, and remove any remaining bones.
3. Bring a separate pan of water to a boil and gently add the eggs. Boil for 8 minutes, then cool in cold water and peel. Chop the eggs finely.
4. Heat the butter in a frying pan over medium heat and sauté the onion until soft. Stir in the curry powder and cook for another minute.
5. Combine the cooked rice, flaked haddock, chopped eggs, sautéed onions, parsley, coriander, lemon zest, and lemon juice in a large bowl. Season the mixture with salt and pepper.
6. Shape the mixture into small bite-sized balls and roll each ball in plain flour.
7. Preheat the air fryer to 190°C.
8. Dip each floured ball into water and then coat with breadcrumbs.
9. Arrange the kedgeree bites in the air fryer basket in a single layer without overcrowding.
10. Air fry for 15 minutes or until golden brown and crispy, turning halfway through the cooking time.
11. Serve warm and enjoy these delightful bites.

NUTRITION FACTS PER 100G:
Energy: 195 kcal | Protein: 10g | Total Fat: 8g | Saturated Fat: 5g
Carbohydrates: 20g | Sugars: 2g | Dietary Fibre: 1g

Avocado and Poached Egg on Toast

SERVINGS: 2 | DIFFICULTY: EASY | TEMPERATURE: 180°C
PREPARATION TIME: 10 MINUTES | COOKING TIME: 10 MINUTES

Ingredients:

* 2 slices of wholegrain bread
* 1 ripe avocado
* 2 eggs
* 1 tbsp olive oil
* a pinch of salt
* a pinch of black pepper
* a handful of fresh coriander, chopped
* 1/2 lemon, juiced

Preparation:

1. Start by preheating the air fryer to 180°C.
2. While the air fryer preheats, cut the avocado in half, remove the pit, and scoop the flesh into a bowl.
3. Mash the avocado with a fork until smooth and stir in the lemon juice, salt, and black pepper.
4. Brush both sides of the bread slices with olive oil.
5. Once the air fryer reaches temperature, place the bread slices in the basket and cook for 5 minutes or until golden and crispy.
6. Meanwhile, bring a small pot of water to a simmer for poaching the eggs.
7. Crack each egg into a small bowl and gently slide into the simmering water.
8. Poach the eggs for about 3 minutes, or until the whites are set but the yolks remain runny.
9. Remove the bread from the air fryer and evenly spread the mashed avocado over each slice.
10. Using a slotted spoon, carefully lift the poached eggs out of the water, allowing any excess water to drain off.
11. Place one poached egg on top of each avocado-covered toast.
12. Garnish generously with chopped coriander and serve immediately.

NUTRITION FACTS PER 100G:
Energy: 230 kcal | Protein: 5g | Total Fat: 18g | Saturated Fat: 3g
Carbohydrates: 13g | Sugars: 1g | Dietary Fibre: 5g

Chapter 2:
Family-Friendly Dinners

Air Fryer Cottage Pie with Crispy Potato Topping

SERVINGS: 4 | DIFFICULTY: MEDIUM | TEMPERATURE: 200°C
PREPARATION TIME: 20 MINUTES | COOKING TIME: 35 MINUTES

Ingredients:

* 500g minced beef
* 1 onion, finely chopped
* 2 carrots, diced
* 2 tbsp tomato puree
* 200ml beef stock
* 1 tbsp Worcestershire sauce
* 1 tsp dried thyme
* salt and pepper to taste
* 700g potatoes, peeled and sliced thinly
* 2 tbsp olive oil
* 50g butter

Preparation:

1. Begin by heating olive oil in a pan over medium heat. Add onions and sauté until translucent.
2. Stir in minced beef and cook until browned. Ensure to break it up as it cooks.
3. Once beef is cooked, add carrots, tomato puree, beef stock, Worcestershire sauce, thyme, salt, and pepper.
4. Allow the mixture to simmer for about 10 minutes, enabling flavours to meld and thicken.
5. Meanwhile, in a separate bowl, toss the potato slices with olive oil, ensuring an even coat.
6. Carefully pour the beef mixture into an air fryer-safe dish, spreading it evenly.
7. Layer the potato slices neatly over the beef mixture, overlapping slightly if necessary.
8. Dot the top with butter and season with a pinch of salt and pepper.
9. Set the air fryer to 200°C and cook the cottage pie for 25-30 minutes, or until the potatoes are golden and crispy.
10. Once cooked, let the cottage pie rest for a few minutes before serving, allowing the juices to settle.

NUTRITION FACTS PER 100G:
Energy: 150 kcal | Protein: 9g | Total Fat: 10g | Saturated Fat: 4g
Carbohydrates: 9g | Sugars: 2g | Dietary Fibre: 1g

Chicken Tikka Masala with Pilau Rice

SERVINGS: 4 | DIFFICULTY: MEDIUM | TEMPERATURE: 200°C
PREPARATION TIME: 30 MINUTES | COOKING TIME: 30 MINUTES

Ingredients:

* 500g chicken breast, cut into cubes
* 100g plain yoghurt
* 2 tbsp lemon juice
* 2 tbsp tandoori masala
* 1 tsp ground cumin
* 1 tsp ground coriander
* 1 tsp turmeric
* 1 tsp garam masala
* salt, to taste
* 1 onion, finely chopped
* 2 cloves garlic, minced
* 1 tbsp ginger, grated
* 400g chopped tomatoes
* 100ml double cream
* 200g basmati rice
* 400ml chicken stock
* 1 tbsp vegetable oil
* fresh coriander, for garnish

Preparation:

1. Begin by marinating the chicken. Combine yoghurt, lemon juice, tandoori masala, ground cumin, ground coriander, turmeric, and salt in a bowl. Add the chicken cubes to this mixture, ensuring they are well-coated. Allow to marinate for at least 15 minutes.

2. Preheat the air fryer to 200°C. Arrange the marinated chicken in a single layer in the air fryer basket. Cook for 12-15 minutes, turning halfway through until the chicken is cooked and slightly charred on the edges.

3. While the chicken is cooking, heat vegetable oil in a pan over medium heat. Sauté the chopped onion until translucent, then stir in the garlic and ginger, cooking for another minute.

4. Pour in the chopped tomatoes and let the mixture simmer for 5-10 minutes until it thickens. Incorporate the garam masala and double cream into the sauce, stirring frequently, and allow it to simmer on low heat.

5. For the pilau rice, rinse the basmati rice under cold water. In a separate pot, bring the chicken stock to a boil. Add the rice to the pot and cover, letting it simmer for approximately 12 minutes, or until the liquid is absorbed and the rice is tender.

6. Once the chicken is done, mix it into the sauce, ensuring all pieces are coated. Garnish with fresh coriander before serving.

7. Serve the chicken tikka masala alongside the pilau rice, and enjoy this delightful dish.

NUTRITION FACTS PER 100G:
Energy: 140 kcal | Protein: 9g | Total Fat: 7g | Saturated Fat: 3g
Carbohydrates: 11g | Sugars: 3g | Dietary Fibre: 1g

Bangers and Mash with Onion Gravy

SERVINGS: 4 | DIFFICULTY: EASY | TEMPERATURE: 180°C
PREPARATION TIME: 15 MINUTES | COOKING TIME: 30 MINUTES

Ingredients:

* 500g pork sausages
* 800g potatoes, peeled and chopped
* 50ml milk
* 50g butter
* 1 large onion, thinly sliced
* 300ml beef stock
* 1 tbsp plain flour
* 1 tbsp Worcestershire sauce
* salt and pepper to taste
* 1 tbsp olive oil

Preparation:

1. Begin by preheating the air fryer to 180°C.
2. Arrange the sausages in the air fryer basket in a single layer. Cook for 12-15 minutes, turning halfway through, until golden brown and cooked through.
3. While the sausages are cooking, prepare the mashed potatoes. Place the chopped potatoes in a large pot, cover with water, and add a pinch of salt. Boil until tender, about 15 minutes.
4. Drain the potatoes and return to the pot. Mash with the butter and milk until smooth. Season with salt and pepper to taste.
5. To prepare the onion gravy, heat the olive oil in a saucepan over medium heat. Add the sliced onion and sauté until caramelised, about 8 minutes.
6. Sprinkle the flour over the onions and stir well. Gradually add the beef stock, stirring continuously to avoid lumps.
7. Stir in the Worcestershire sauce and simmer on low heat for 5 minutes until thickened. Season with salt and pepper.
8. Serve the sausages over a generous portion of mash and drizzle with onion gravy.

NUTRITION FACTS PER 100G:
Energy: 137 kcal | Protein: 4g | Total Fat: 9g | Saturated Fat: 3g
Carbohydrates: 11g | Sugars: 1g | Dietary Fibre: 2g

Roast Beef with Yorkshire Puddings

SERVINGS: 4 | DIFFICULTY: MEDIUM | TEMPERATURE: 180°C
PREPARATION TIME: 20 MINUTES | COOKING TIME: 60 MINUTES

Ingredients:

* 800g beef top round roast
* 2 tbsp olive oil
* 2 tsp sea salt
* 1 tsp black pepper
* 1 tsp dried thyme
* 1 tsp garlic powder
* 120g plain flour
* 2 large eggs
* 150ml milk
* 50ml water
* 50ml vegetable oil

Preparation:

1. Begin by preheating the air fryer to 180°C.
2. For the beef, rub olive oil all over the roast. Combine sea salt, black pepper, dried thyme, and garlic powder, then season the beef thoroughly.
3. Place the beef in the air fryer basket, ensuring it's centred. Cook for 45 minutes, turning halfway through the cooking time for even browning.
4. While the beef roasts, prepare the batter for Yorkshire puddings. In a bowl, whisk the eggs, flour, milk, and water until smooth. Allow the batter to rest for 15 minutes.
5. Once the beef is cooked, remove it from the air fryer and let it rest, wrapped in foil, for approximately 10 minutes.
6. Increase the air fryer temperature to 200°C.
7. In each compartment of a silicone muffin moulds, pour about 1 tsp of vegetable oil. Place the moulds in the air fryer for 3 minutes to heat the oil.
8. Quickly pour the prepared batter into the hot oil, filling each mould about halfway.
9. Cook the Yorkshire puddings for 12-15 minutes or until they are puffed up and golden brown.
10. Serve the roast beef sliced, accompanied by the fluffy Yorkshire puddings.

NUTRITION FACTS PER 100G:
Energy: 239 kcal | Protein: 16g | Total Fat: 15g | Saturated Fat: 3g
Carbohydrates: 12g | Sugars: 1g | Dietary Fibre: 1g

Shepherd's Pie with a Golden Crust

SERVINGS: 4 | DIFFICULTY: MEDIUM | TEMPERATURE: 200°C
PREPARATION TIME: 20 MINUTES | COOKING TIME: 35 MINUTES

Ingredients:

* 500g minced lamb
* 1 onion, finely chopped
* 2 carrots, diced
* 150g frozen peas
* 2 tbsp tomato purée
* 1 tbsp Worcestershire sauce
* 1 tbsp plain flour
* 250ml beef stock
* 600g potatoes, peeled and cut into chunks
* 50ml milk
* 2 tbsp butter
* 1 tbsp olive oil
* salt and pepper, to taste

Preparation:

1. Begin by peeling the potatoes and cutting them into chunks. Boil them in salted water until tender.
2. As the potatoes cook, heat olive oil in a pan over medium heat. Sauté the chopped onion and carrots until they soften.
3. Add the minced lamb to the pan, cooking until browned.
4. Stir in the tomato purée, Worcestershire sauce, and plain flour, ensuring everything is well combined.
5. Gradually pour in the beef stock, stirring continuously until the mixture thickens.
6. Incorporate the frozen peas, seasoning with salt and pepper as desired. Simmer for 5 minutes.
7. Once the potatoes are soft, drain and mash with butter and milk until smooth. Season with salt and pepper.
8. Preheat the air fryer to 200°C.
9. Transfer the meat mixture into a suitable air fryer dish and spread the mashed potatoes evenly on top.
10. Cook in the air fryer for 20 minutes, or until the top is golden and crisp.
11. Allow to cool slightly before serving.

NUTRITION FACTS PER 100G:
Energy: 130 kcal | Protein: 7g | Total Fat: 7g | Saturated Fat: 3g
Carbohydrates: 10g | Sugars: 1g | Dietary Fibre: 1g

Lamb Koftas with Mint Yoghurt Dip

SERVINGS: 4 | DIFFICULTY: MEDIUM | TEMPERATURE: 180°C
PREPARATION TIME: 20 MINUTES | COOKING TIME: 15 MINUTES

Ingredients:

* 500g lamb mince
* 1 onion, finely chopped
* 2 garlic cloves, minced
* 1 tsp ground cumin
* 1 tsp ground coriander
* 1 tsp paprika
* 1 tsp salt
* 1/2 tsp black pepper

* 2 tbsp fresh parsley, chopped
* 2 tbsp olive oil

Mint Yoghurt Dip:

* 200ml natural yoghurt
* 2 tbsp fresh mint, chopped
* 1 tbsp lemon juice
* 1/2 tsp salt
* 1/4 tsp black pepper

Preparation:

1. Begin by combining the lamb mince, onion, garlic, cumin, ground coriander, paprika, salt, black pepper, and fresh parsley in a large bowl.
2. Mix the ingredients thoroughly until well combined, taking care to ensure spices are evenly distributed.
3. Shape the mixture into small, cylindrical koftas, each approximately 7–8cm in length.
4. Brush each kofta lightly with olive oil to ensure a crispy exterior.
5. Preheat your air fryer to 180°C for 3 minutes.
6. Place the koftas in the air fryer basket, ensuring they are not overcrowded.
7. Cook for 15 minutes, turning halfway through, until browned and cooked through.
8. While the koftas are cooking, prepare the mint yoghurt dip by mixing the natural yoghurt, fresh mint, lemon juice, salt, and black pepper in a bowl.
9. Stir until all ingredients are fully combined and the dip is smooth.
10. Once the koftas are cooked, remove them from the air fryer and serve immediately with the mint yoghurt dip on the side.

NUTRITION FACTS PER 100G:
Energy: 235 kcal | Protein: 15g | Total Fat: 18g | Saturated Fat: 6g
Carbohydrates: 4g | Sugars: 2g | Dietary Fibre: 1g

Crispy Breaded Haddock with Chips

SERVINGS: 2 | DIFFICULTY: MEDIUM | TEMPERATURE: 200°C
PREPARATION TIME: 15 MINUTES | COOKING TIME: 20 MINUTES

Ingredients:

* 2 haddock fillets (approx. 150g each)
* 150g breadcrumbs
* 50g plain flour
* 1 egg
* 1 tsp paprika
* salt and pepper to taste
* 300g potatoes, cut into chips
* 2 tbsp olive oil
* 1 lemon, cut into wedges
* Tartare sauce, for serving

Preparation:

1. Begin by preheating your air fryer to 200°C.
2. In a shallow dish, combine breadcrumbs, paprika, salt, and pepper.
3. Place flour in a separate plate.
4. Beat the egg in a bowl.
5. Dredge each haddock fillet in flour, then dip in the beaten egg, ensuring it's well-coated.
6. Press the fillets into the breadcrumb mixture, covering completely.
7. Toss potato chips with olive oil, salt, and pepper in a large bowl.
8. Arrange potato chips in the air fryer basket and cook for 10 minutes, shaking halfway.
9. Carefully place breaded haddock fillets in the air fryer, alongside the chips, and cook for an additional 10 minutes.
10. Verify that haddock is cooked through and golden brown.
11. Serve immediately with lemon wedges and tartare sauce on the side.

NUTRITION FACTS PER 100G:
Energy: 168 kcal | Protein: 10g | Total Fat: 7g | Saturated Fat: 1g
Carbohydrates: 20g | Sugars: 1g | Dietary Fibre: 2g

Chicken and Mushroom Pie with Puff Pastry

SERVINGS: 4 | DIFFICULTY: MEDIUM | TEMPERATURE: 200°C
PREPARATION TIME: 20 MINUTES | COOKING TIME: 25 MINUTES

Ingredients:

* 500g chicken breast, diced
* 200g chestnut mushrooms, sliced
* 1 onion, finely chopped
* 2 cloves garlic, minced
* 1 tbsp olive oil
* 1 tbsp plain flour
* 150ml chicken stock
* 100ml double cream
* 1 tsp dried thyme
* salt and pepper, to taste
* 320g puff pastry sheet, ready-rolled
* 1 egg, beaten (for glaze)

Preparation:

1. Initially, heat the olive oil in a pan over medium heat. Sauté the onion and garlic until softened.
2. Add the chicken cubes to the pan and cook until they are golden on all sides.
3. Introduce the sliced mushrooms and cook for a further 3-4 minutes, allowing them to soften.
4. Sprinkle the flour over the mixture and stir well to coat the chicken and mushrooms.
5. Gradually pour in the chicken stock and double cream, stirring continuously, and bring to a gentle simmer.
6. Season with thyme, salt, and pepper, stirring the mixture occasionally until it thickens. Remove from heat and let it cool slightly.
7. Roll out the puff pastry on a lightly floured surface. Cut the pastry into rounds that fit your air fryer basket.
8. Spoon the chicken and mushroom mixture evenly onto half of the pastry circles, leaving a gap around the edges.
9. Brush the beaten egg along the edges of the filled pastry circles. Place another circle on top and press the edges together to seal the pies.
10. Brush the tops of the pies with the remaining beaten egg to ensure a golden finish.
11. Preheat your air fryer to 200°C. Place the pies in the basket, ensuring they are not touching, and cook for 12-15 minutes until the pastry is crisp and golden brown.
12. Once done, carefully remove the pies from the air fryer and let them cool slightly before serving.

NUTRITION FACTS PER 100G:
Energy: 260 kcal | Protein: 9g | Total Fat: 17g | Saturated Fat: 8g
Carbohydrates: 18g | Sugars: 2g | Dietary Fibre: 1g

Air Fryer Sausage Rolls with Mustard

SERVINGS: 4 | DIFFICULTY: EASY | TEMPERATURE: 180°C
PREPARATION TIME: 15 MINUTES | COOKING TIME: 20 MINUTES

Ingredients:

* 1 sheet of ready-rolled puff pastry (approximately 320g)
* 300g pork sausage meat
* 1 tbsp wholegrain mustard
* 1 egg yolk
* salt and pepper to taste
* 1 tbsp milk (for egg wash)
* 1 tsp dried thyme

Preparation:

1. Begin by preheating the air fryer to 180°C.
2. Unroll the puff pastry sheet on a clean surface.
3. In a bowl, combine the pork sausage meat, wholegrain mustard, dried thyme, salt, and pepper.
4. Carefully spread the sausage mixture down one edge of the pastry, leaving a small border.
5. Gently roll the pastry over the sausage meat, sealing the edges with a bit of water.
6. Cut the rolled pastry into approximately 8 equally sized pieces.
7. Whisk together the egg yolk and milk to create an egg wash.
8. Lightly brush the top of each sausage roll with the egg wash to ensure a golden finish.
9. Arrange the sausage rolls in the air fryer basket, making sure they are not overcrowded.
10. Cook for 20 minutes or until the pastry is puffed and golden brown.
11. Once cooked, remove the sausage rolls from the air fryer and let them cool slightly before serving.

NUTRITION FACTS PER 100G:
Energy: 320 kcal | Protein: 8g | Total Fat: 22g | Saturated Fat: 9g
Carbohydrates: 21g | Sugars: 2g | Dietary Fibre: 1g

Roast Chicken with Herby Potatoes

SERVINGS: 4 | DIFFICULTY: MEDIUM | TEMPERATURE: 180°C
PREPARATION TIME: 15 MINUTES | COOKING TIME: 40 MINUTES

Ingredients:

* 1 whole chicken (approx. 1.5kg)
* 500g baby potatoes, halved
* 3 tbsp olive oil
* 2 tbsp fresh rosemary, chopped
* 1 tbsp fresh thyme, chopped
* 4 garlic cloves, minced
* 1 lemon, halved
* salt and pepper to taste

Preparation:

1. Begin by patting the chicken dry with kitchen paper and season the cavity with salt and pepper.
2. Squeeze the juice of half a lemon over the chicken, then place the squeezed lemon half inside the cavity along with half of the rosemary and thyme.
3. Stir together 2 tbsp of olive oil with the minced garlic and remaining herbs in a small bowl.
4. Carefully loosen the skin over the chicken breast and rub the herb mixture underneath the skin.
5. Arrange the halved potatoes in a bowl and toss them with the remaining olive oil, and season with salt and pepper.
6. Preheat the air fryer to 180°C for about 3 minutes.
7. Place the seasoned chicken in the air fryer basket, ensuring there is space around it for even cooking.
8. Scatter the prepared potatoes around the chicken in the basket.
9. Cook in the air fryer for approximately 40 minutes, or until the chicken reaches an internal temperature of 75°C, and the potatoes are tender and golden.
10. Once cooked, remove from the air fryer and let the chicken rest for 5 minutes before carving. Serve alongside the herby potatoes.

NUTRITION FACTS PER 100G:
Energy: 150kcal | Protein: 16g | Total Fat: 8g | Saturated Fat: 2g
Carbohydrates: 5g | Sugars: 1g | Dietary Fibre: 1g

Beef Wellington Bites

SERVINGS: 4 | DIFFICULTY: MEDIUM | TEMPERATURE: 180°C
PREPARATION TIME: 30 MINUTES | COOKING TIME: 15 MINUTES

Ingredients:

- 500g beef fillet, cut into small cubes
- 1 sheet puff pastry, thawed
- 100g chestnut mushrooms, finely chopped
- 1 small shallot, finely chopped
- 2 tbsp olive oil
- 1 tbsp English mustard
- 1 egg, beaten
- salt and black pepper, to taste
- 50g pâté
- 1 tbsp fresh parsley, finely chopped

Preparation:

1. Start by heating 1tbsp of olive oil in a pan over medium heat. Cook the shallot and mushrooms until softened and moisture has evaporated, about 5 minutes.
2. Remove the mushroom mixture from heat and let it cool. Once cooled, mix in the parsley and season with salt and pepper.
3. In the same pan, sear the beef cubes with the remaining olive oil over high heat briefly, about 1 minute per side. Aim for a nice sear; they'll cook further in the air fryer.
4. Brush each beef cube with English mustard, then spread a thin layer of pâté over each one.
5. Prepare the puff pastry by rolling it out slightly on a floured surface. Cut the pastry into squares large enough to envelop each beef cube.
6. Place a piece of beef, pâté side down, onto a pastry square. Add a teaspoon of mushroom mixture on top, then fold the pastry over, sealing the edges with a little beaten egg.
7. Repeat the wrapping process with the remaining beef cubes and pastry squares.
8. Preheat your air fryer to 180°C.
9. Brush each wrapped bite with the beaten egg, ensuring a golden finish after cooking.
10. Arrange the Beef Wellington bites in the air fryer basket in a single layer. You may need to cook them in batches depending on your air fryer's size.
11. Air fry for 12-15 minutes until the pastry turns a golden brown and crisps up.
12. Allow the bites to cool slightly before serving.

> **NUTRITION FACTS PER 100G:**
> Energy: 270 kcal | Protein: 14g | Total Fat: 18g | Saturated Fat: 6g
> Carbohydrates: 17g | Sugars: 1g | Dietary Fibre: 1g

Gammon Steaks with Pineapple

SERVINGS: 2 | DIFFICULTY: EASY | TEMPERATURE: 180°C
PREPARATION TIME: 10 MINUTES | COOKING TIME: 15 MINUTES

Ingredients:

* 2g gammon steaks (approx. 200g each)
* 4 pineapple rings (canned or fresh)
* 1 tbsp olive oil
* 1 tbsp honey
* 1 tbsp soy sauce
* 1/2 tsp black pepper
* 1/2 tsp paprika
* 1/2 tsp garlic powder
* lemon wedges, for serving

Preparation:

1. Begin by preheating your air fryer to 180°C.
2. In a small bowl, mix together the olive oil, honey, soy sauce, black pepper, paprika, and garlic powder to create a marinade.
3. Brush the gammon steaks generously with the marinade and let them sit for a few minutes to absorb the flavours.
4. Place the gammon steaks in the air fryer basket, ensuring they are not overlapping.
5. Air fry the gammon steaks for 10 minutes, flipping them halfway through for even cooking.
6. In the last 5 minutes, add the pineapple rings to the air fryer, placing them alongside the gammon steaks.
7. Once the gammon steaks are cooked through and the pineapple is slightly caramelised, remove them from the air fryer.
8. Serve the gammon steaks and pineapple rings hot, garnished with lemon wedges for an added zest.

NUTRITION FACTS PER 100G:
Energy: 172 kcal | Protein: 15g | Total Fat: 8g | Saturated Fat: 2g
Carbohydrates: 10g | Sugars: 8g | Dietary Fibre: 1g

Toad in the Hole with Gravy

SERVINGS: 4 | DIFFICULTY: MEDIUM | TEMPERATURE: 200°C
PREPARATION TIME: 15 MINUTES | COOKING TIME: 30 MINUTES

Ingredients:

* 200g plain flour
* 250ml whole milk
* 3 large eggs
* 1 tbsp mustard
* 1 tbsp vegetable oil
* 6 pork sausages
* salt and pepper, to taste

For the Gravy:

* 1 large onion, thinly sliced
* 2 tbsp unsalted butter
* 1 tbsp plain flour
* 250ml beef stock
* 1 tbsp Worcestershire sauce
* salt and pepper, to taste

Preparation:

1. Begin by preheating your air fryer to 200°C.
2. In a mixing bowl, whisk together the flour, milk, eggs, mustard, salt, and pepper to form a smooth batter. Let it rest for 10 minutes.
3. Scatter the vegetable oil at the bottom of the air fryer pan, then add the sausages.
4. Cook the sausages in the air fryer for 8 minutes until they are browned.
5. Carefully pour the batter over the sausages, ensuring they are evenly covered.
6. Continue cooking for an additional 20 minutes or until the batter has risen and is golden.
7. Meanwhile, prepare the gravy by melting butter in a saucepan over medium heat.
8. Sauté the sliced onions until they are soft and caramelised.
9. Stir in the flour and cook for a minute to form a roux.
10. Gradually add the beef stock while stirring continuously, allowing the gravy to thicken.
11. Mix in the Worcestershire sauce and season with salt and pepper to taste.
12. Once the toad in the hole is cooked, remove from the air fryer, slice, and serve hot with the onion gravy.

NUTRITION FACTS PER 100G:
Energy: 185 kcal | Protein: 7g | Total Fat: 12g | Saturated Fat: 4g
Carbohydrates: 13g | Sugars: 3g | Dietary Fibre: 1g

Fish Finger Butties with Tartare Sauce

SERVINGS: 4 | DIFFICULTY: EASY | TEMPERATURE: 200°C
PREPARATION TIME: 15 MINUTES | COOKING TIME: 20 MINUTES

Ingredients:

- 400g white fish fillets (such as cod or haddock), cut into strips
- 100g plain flour
- 2 eggs, beaten
- 150g breadcrumbs
- 1 tsp salt
- 1/2 tsp black pepper
- 4 soft bread rolls
- 2 tbsp butter
- 2 tbsp mayonnaise
- 1 tbsp capers, chopped
- 2 gherkins, finely chopped
- 1 tbsp lemon juice
- 1 tbsp fresh parsley, chopped
- lettuce leaves

Preparation:

1. Preheat your air fryer to 200°C for a few minutes.
2. Season the fish fillets with salt and pepper.
3. Set up a dredging station with three bowls: the first with flour, the second with beaten eggs, and the third with breadcrumbs.
4. Coat each fish strip in flour, shake off the excess, dip in the beaten eggs, and finally coat with breadcrumbs.
5. Arrange the breaded fish fingers in the air fryer basket, ensuring they are not overcrowded.
6. Cook the fish fingers for 15-20 minutes, turning halfway through, until golden and cooked through.
7. While the fish is cooking, prepare the tartare sauce by combining mayonnaise, capers, gherkins, lemon juice, and parsley in a small bowl.
8. Slightly warm the bread rolls and spread with butter.
9. Once the fish fingers are done, place lettuce leaves on the bottom half of the rolls, followed by the fish fingers.
10. Generously spoon tartare sauce over the fish, then top with the other half of the bread roll. Serve immediately.

NUTRITION FACTS PER 100G:
Energy: 215 kcal | Protein: 12g | Total Fat: 9g | Saturated Fat: 3g
Carbohydrates: 22g | Sugars: 2g | Dietary Fibre: 1g

Steak and Kidney Pudding

SERVINGS: 4 | DIFFICULTY: MEDIUM | TEMPERATURE: 180°C
PREPARATION TIME: 30 MINUTES | COOKING TIME: 1 HOUR 30 MINUTES

Ingredients:

* 300g beef steak, diced
* 200g lamb kidney, diced
* 200g plain flour
* 100g suet
* 1 onion, finely chopped
* 250ml beef stock
* 1 tbsp Worcestershire sauce
* 1 tbsp vegetable oil
* salt and pepper to taste
* 1 egg, beaten

Preparation:

1. Begin by preparing the suet crust. In a mixing bowl, combine the plain flour and suet. Gradually add cold water until a soft dough forms.
2. Roll out two-thirds of the dough on a floured surface to line a greased pudding mould. Retain the remaining dough for the lid.
3. Heat vegetable oil in a frying pan and sauté the onion until translucent.
4. Add the beef steak and lamb kidney to the pan. Brown the meat evenly.
5. Stir in the Worcestershire sauce, beef stock, salt, and pepper, cooking until the mixture thickens slightly.
6. Spoon the steak and kidney filling into the dough-lined pudding mould.
7. Roll out the remaining dough and place it over the top of the filling, sealing the edges firmly.
8. Brush the top with beaten egg.
9. Gently place the pudding mould into the air fryer basket.
10. Set the air fryer to 180°C and cook for 1 hour and 30 minutes.
11. Once cooked, allow the pudding to cool slightly before turning it out onto a serving plate.
12. Cut into portions and serve hot.

NUTRITION FACTS PER 100G:
Energy: 215 kcal | Protein: 13g | Total Fat: 14g | Saturated Fat: 6g
Carbohydrates: 11g | Sugars: 1g | Dietary Fibre: 1g

Chicken and Leek Hotpot

SERVINGS: 4 | DIFFICULTY: MEDIUM | TEMPERATURE: 180°C
PREPARATION TIME: 15 MINUTES | COOKING TIME: 40 MINUTES

Ingredients:

* 500g chicken breast, diced
* 2 medium leeks, sliced
* 200g potatoes, thinly sliced
* 150ml chicken stock
* 100ml double cream

* 2 tbsp olive oil
* 1 tsp dried thyme
* salt and pepper to taste
* 1 tbsp cornflour
* 1 tbsp water

Preparation:

1. Begin by preheating the air fryer to 180°C.
2. Meanwhile, in a bowl, combine the diced chicken, olive oil, thyme, salt, and pepper. Mix well to coat.
3. Transfer the seasoned chicken into the air fryer basket and cook for 15 minutes, turning halfway through.
4. As the chicken cooks, blend the cornflour with water to create a smooth paste. Set aside.
5. In a separate pan, heat a little olive oil over medium heat and sauté the leeks until they are soft.
6. Pour in the chicken stock and bring to a simmer, then stir in the double cream.
7. Add the cornflour mixture to the creamy leeks, stirring continuously until the sauce thickens.
8. Once the chicken is ready, combine it with the creamy leek sauce and mix well.
9. Layer the sliced potatoes in the bottom of an oven-safe dish that fits your air fryer, then pour the chicken and leek mixture over the top.
10. Place the dish into the air fryer basket and cook for an additional 25 minutes, or until the potatoes are tender and the top is golden.
11. Allow the hotpot to cool slightly before serving.

NUTRITION FACTS PER 100G:
Energy: 135 kcal | Protein: 10g | Total Fat: 9g | Saturated Fat: 4g
Carbohydrates: 6g | Sugars: 2g | Dietary Fibre: 1g

Pork Belly Bites with Apple Sauce

SERVINGS: 4 | DIFFICULTY: MEDIUM | TEMPERATURE: 180°C
PREPARATION TIME: 20 MINUTES | COOKING TIME: 25 MINUTES

Ingredients:

* 600g pork belly, cut into bite-sized pieces
* 1 tbsp olive oil
* 1 tsp sea salt
* 1/2 tsp black pepper
* 1 tsp smoked paprika
* 150g apples, peeled and chopped
* 50ml apple cider
* 1 tbsp sugar
* 1/2 tsp cinnamon
* 1/2 tsp lemon juice

Preparation:

1. Start by preheating your air fryer to 180°C.
2. In a bowl, combine the pork belly bites with olive oil, sea salt, black pepper, and smoked paprika. Mix well to coat the pork evenly.
3. Place the seasoned pork belly pieces in the air fryer basket in a single layer. Cook for 20 minutes, shaking the basket halfway through.
4. While the pork is cooking, prepare the apple sauce by placing the chopped apples, apple cider, sugar, and cinnamon in a saucepan over medium heat.
5. Cook the apple mixture for approximately 10 minutes, stirring occasionally, until the apples are tender and the sauce has thickened.
6. Blend the apple mixture until smooth, then stir in the lemon juice to enhance the flavour.
7. Once the pork belly bites are crispy and golden, remove from the air fryer.
8. Serve the pork belly bites hot with the freshly prepared apple sauce on the side.

NUTRITION FACTS PER 100G:
Energy: 242 kcal | Protein: 9g | Total Fat: 20g | Saturated Fat: 7g
Carbohydrates: 6g | Sugars: 3g | Dietary Fibre: 1g

Beef and Ale Pie with Crispy Pastry

SERVINGS: 4 | DIFFICULTY: MEDIUM | TEMPERATURE: 180°C
PREPARATION TIME: 30 MINUTES | COOKING TIME: 1 HOUR 15 MINUTES

Ingredients:

* 500g beef stewing steak, diced
* 1 tbsp olive oil
* 1 onion, finely chopped
* 2 cloves garlic, minced
* 200ml ale
* 200ml beef stock
* 2 tbsp plain flour
* 1 tsp Worcestershire sauce
* 1 tbsp tomato purée
* 1 carrot, diced
* 1 tsp thyme
* salt and pepper, to taste
* 300g ready-rolled puff pastry
* 1 egg, beaten

Preparation:

1. Begin by preheating your air fryer to 180°C.
2. In a large pan, heat the olive oil and brown the beef in batches, then remove and set aside.
3. Sauté the onion and garlic until softened.
4. Stir in the flour and cook for 1 minute.
5. Gradually add the ale and beef stock, stirring constantly.
6. Return the beef to the pan, adding Worcestershire sauce, tomato purée, carrot, thyme, salt, and pepper.
7. Simmer gently for 45 minutes until the beef is tender.
8. Roll out the puff pastry and cut to fit your air fryer baking dish.
9. Pour the beef mixture into the dish and cover with the pastry, sealing the edges.
10. Brush the pastry with the beaten egg.
11. Place the pie in the air fryer and cook for 30 minutes or until the pastry is golden and crispy.
12. Allow to cool for a few minutes before serving.

NUTRITION FACTS PER 100G:
Energy: 190 kcal | Protein: 8g | Total Fat: 12g | Saturated Fat: 4g
Carbohydrates: 11g | Sugars: 1g | Dietary Fibre: 1g

Battered Cod with Chunky Chips

SERVINGS: 4 | DIFFICULTY: MEDIUM | TEMPERATURE: 200°C
PREPARATION TIME: 20 MINUTES | COOKING TIME: 25 MINUTES

Ingredients:

* 500g cod fillets
* 300g potatoes
* 100g plain flour
* 1 tsp baking powder
* 200ml cold sparkling water
* 1 tbsp olive oil
* salt, to taste
* pepper, to taste
* Lemon wedges, to serve

Preparation:

1. Begin by peeling the potatoes and cutting them into chunky chips. Rinse under cold water to remove excess starch.
2. Pat the chips dry using a clean kitchen towel and then coat evenly with olive oil, salt, and pepper.
3. Preheat the air fryer to 200°C and arrange the chips in a single layer in the basket. Cook for 15 minutes, shaking halfway through, until golden and crispy.
4. While the chips are cooking, prepare the batter. In a mixing bowl, combine plain flour, baking powder, a pinch of salt, and a touch of pepper.
5. Gradually whisk in the sparkling water until a smooth batter forms. Set aside to let it rest briefly.
6. Pat the cod fillets dry with kitchen paper and lightly season with salt and pepper.
7. Dip each fillet into the batter, ensuring it's fully coated.
8. Once the chips are done, remove them from the air fryer and keep warm.
9. Place the battered cod fillets in the air fryer basket, ensuring they do not touch, and cook at 200°C for 10 minutes, turning halfway through.
10. Check the fillets for a golden brown crust and ensure the fish is cooked through.
11. Serve the battered cod with the chunky chips and lemon wedges on the side.

NUTRITION FACTS PER 100G:
Energy: 160 kcal | Protein: 11g | Total Fat: 3g | Saturated Fat: 1g
Carbohydrates: 24g | Sugars: 1g | Dietary Fibre: 1g

Cornish Pasties with Steak Filling

SERVINGS: 4 | DIFFICULTY: MEDIUM | TEMPERATURE: 180°C
PREPARATION TIME: 30 MINUTES | COOKING TIME: 20 MINUTES

Ingredients:

* 400g beef steak, finely diced
* 200g potatoes, peeled and finely diced
* 100g swede, peeled and finely diced
* 1 medium onion, finely chopped
* 1 tbsp fresh parsley, chopped
* salt, to taste
* black pepper, to taste
* 500g shortcrust pastry
* 1 egg, beaten

Preparation:

1. Begin by combining the beef steak, potatoes, swede, onion, and parsley together in a large bowl. Season generously with salt and black pepper.
2. Roll out the shortcrust pastry on a floured surface to about 5mm thick and cut into 4 circles (approximately 20cm in diameter).
3. Divide the filling evenly among the pastry circles. Place it on one half of each circle, leaving a small border around the edge.
4. Brush the edges of the pastry with beaten egg, fold the other half over the filling to form a semi-circle, and crimp the edges to seal the pasties securely.
5. Preheat the air fryer to 180°C.
6. Once heated, carefully place the pasties in the air fryer basket, ensuring they do not touch each other.
7. Brush the tops of the pasties with the remaining beaten egg.
8. Cook in the air fryer for about 20 minutes or until golden brown and crisp on the outside.
9. Carefully remove from the air fryer and allow to cool slightly before serving.

NUTRITION FACTS PER 100G:
Energy: 234 kcal | Protein: 9g | Total Fat: 14g | Saturated Fat: 6g
Carbohydrates: 20g | Sugars: 1g | Dietary Fibre: 1g

Chapter 3:
Light and Healthy Lunches

Grilled Halloumi and Aubergine Salad

Ingredients:

* 200g halloumi cheese, sliced
* 1 medium aubergine, sliced
* 100g cherry tomatoes, halved
* 50g mixed salad leaves
* 2 tbsp extra virgin olive oil
* 1 tbsp lemon juice
* 1 tsp dried oregano
* salt and pepper to taste
* 2 tbsp pine nuts, toasted
* fresh basil leaves for garnish

Preparation:

1. Begin by preheating your air fryer to 180°C.
2. Drizzle the aubergine slices with 1tbsp of olive oil, ensuring they are evenly coated.
3. Place the aubergine slices in the air fryer basket. Cook for 5 minutes, turning them halfway through.
4. Once the aubergine is done, remove it and set aside. Add the halloumi slices to the air fryer and cook for another 5 minutes until golden brown.
5. In a large bowl, combine the mixed salad leaves, cherry tomatoes, and cooked aubergine.
6. Whisk together the remaining olive oil, lemon juice, oregano, salt, and pepper to create a dressing.
7. Pour the dressing over the salad and toss gently to coat.
8. Arrange the grilled halloumi on top of the salad.
9. Sprinkle with toasted pine nuts and garnish with fresh basil leaves.
10. Serve immediately and enjoy your delicious grilled halloumi and aubergine salad!

NUTRITION FACTS PER 100G:
Energy: 201kcal | Protein: 9g | Total Fat: 16g | Saturated Fat: 7g
Carbohydrates: 5g | Sugars: 3g | Dietary Fibre: 2g

Air Fryer Jacket Potatoes with Cottage Cheese

SERVINGS: 4 | DIFFICULTY: EASY | TEMPERATURE: 200°C
PREPARATION TIME: 10 MINUTES | COOKING TIME: 35 MINUTES

Ingredients:

* 4 medium potatoes (around 200g each)
* 1 tbsp olive oil
* salt, to taste
* black pepper, to taste
* 200g cottage cheese
* 2 tbsp fresh chives, chopped
* 1 tbsp lemon juice
* 1 tsp garlic powder

Preparation:

1. Begin by washing the potatoes thoroughly and pat them dry with a clean towel.
2. Using a fork, prick the potatoes several times all over their surfaces.
3. Coat the potatoes with olive oil, ensuring they are evenly covered.
4. Season generously with salt and black pepper.
5. Preheat your air fryer to 200°C.
6. Arrange the potatoes in the air fryer basket, ensuring they are not overcrowded.
7. Cook the potatoes for 35 minutes, turning them halfway through the cooking time to ensure even crisping.
8. In a mixing bowl, combine the cottage cheese, chopped chives, lemon juice, garlic powder, and a pinch of salt and pepper.
9. Once the potatoes are cooked and the skins are crispy, remove them from the air fryer.
10. Slice each potato open lengthwise and fluff the interior with a fork.
11. Divide the cottage cheese mixture among the potatoes, spooning it into the fluffy centres.
12. Serve immediately for the best experience.

NUTRITION FACTS PER 100G:
Energy: 109 kcal | Protein: 3g | Total Fat: 4g | Saturated Fat: 1g
Carbohydrates: 16g | Sugars: 1g | Dietary Fibre: 2g

Roast Veggie Wrap with Hummus

SERVINGS: 4 | DIFFICULTY: EASY | TEMPERATURE: 190°C
PREPARATION TIME: 15 MINUTES | COOKING TIME: 20 MINUTES

Ingredients:

* 1 red pepper, sliced
* 1 yellow pepper, sliced
* 1 courgette, sliced
* 1 red onion, sliced
* 100g cherry tomatoes, halved
* 1 aubergine, diced
* 2 tbsp olive oil
* 1 tsp mixed herbs
* salt and pepper to taste
* 200g hummus
* 4 whole wheat wraps
* handful of rocket leaves
* lemon wedges for serving

Preparation:

1. Begin by preheating your air fryer to 190°C.
2. In a large bowl, combine the red pepper, yellow pepper, courgette, red onion, cherry tomatoes, and aubergine.
3. Drizzle the vegetables with olive oil and season with mixed herbs, salt, and pepper.
4. Toss the vegetables until evenly coated with the oil and seasonings.
5. Place the vegetables into the air fryer basket, ensuring they are spread out evenly.
6. Cook them in the air fryer for 15 to 18 minutes, or until they are tender and slightly caramelised, shaking the basket halfway through.
7. Once cooked, remove the vegetables from the air fryer and set them aside.
8. Spread a generous amount of hummus onto each whole wheat wrap.
9. Add the roasted vegetables and a handful of rocket leaves on top of the hummus.
10. Roll up the wraps tightly, securing them with a toothpick if necessary.
11. Serve the wraps with lemon wedges for an added zest and enjoy your healthy meal!

NUTRITION FACTS PER 100G:
Energy: 150 kcal | Protein: 4g | Total Fat: 7g | Saturated Fat: 1g
Carbohydrates: 16g | Sugars: 4g | Dietary Fibre: 4g

Prawn and Avocado Salad with Lemon Dressing

SERVINGS: 4 | DIFFICULTY: EASY | TEMPERATURE: 200°C
PREPARATION TIME: 15 MINUTES | COOKING TIME: 10 MINUTES

Ingredients:

* 400g prawns, peeled and deveined
* 2 ripe avocados, diced
* 150g mixed salad leaves
* 100g cherry tomatoes, halved
* 1 small red onion, thinly sliced
* 3 tbsp olive oil
* 2 tbsp lemon juice
* 1 tsp lemon zest
* 1 clove garlic, minced
* salt, to taste
* black pepper, to taste

Preparation:

1. Preheat the air fryer to 200°C.
2. In a small bowl, whisk together the olive oil, lemon juice, lemon zest, minced garlic, salt, and black pepper to create the dressing.
3. Place the prawns in a medium-sized bowl and toss them with 1 tablespoon of the prepared dressing.
4. Arrange the prawns in the air fryer basket, ensuring they are in a single layer. Cook for 8-10 minutes, shaking the basket halfway through until they are pink and cooked through.
5. While the prawns are cooking, combine the mixed salad leaves, diced avocados, cherry tomatoes, and sliced red onion in a large salad bowl.
6. Once the prawns are cooked, add them to the salad and drizzle with the remaining lemon dressing.
7. Gently toss the salad to combine all ingredients thoroughly.
8. Serve immediately, ensuring each plate gets an even amount of salad and prawns.

NUTRITION FACTS PER 100G:
Energy: 160 kcal | Protein: 9g | Total Fat: 13g | Saturated Fat: 2g
Carbohydrates: 4g | Sugars: 1g | Dietary Fibre: 1g

Butternut Squash and Quinoa Salad

SERVINGS: 4 | DIFFICULTY: MEDIUM | TEMPERATURE: 200°C
PREPARATION TIME: 15 MINUTES | COOKING TIME: 25 MINUTES

Ingredients:

* 400g butternut squash, peeled and diced
* 2 tbsp olive oil
* 1 tsp ground cumin
* 150g quinoa
* 500ml vegetable stock
* 100g cherry tomatoes, halved
* 50g feta cheese, crumbled
* 2 tbsp pumpkin seeds
* small bunch of fresh coriander, chopped
* juice of 1 lemon
* salt and black pepper to taste

Preparation:

1. Preheat the air fryer to 200°C.
2. In a large bowl, toss the diced butternut squash with olive oil, ground cumin, salt, and black pepper until well coated.
3. Arrange the seasoned squash in the air fryer basket in a single layer and cook for 20 minutes or until tender and golden, shaking halfway through.
4. Meanwhile, rinse the quinoa under cold water, then place it in a pot with the vegetable stock. Bring to a boil, cover, and simmer for 15 minutes until the liquid is absorbed and the quinoa is fluffy.
5. Once the butternut squash is cooked, allow it to cool slightly before combining it in a large salad bowl with the cooked quinoa.
6. Add the halved cherry tomatoes, crumbled feta cheese, and pumpkin seeds to the bowl.
7. Drizzle the salad with lemon juice, then gently fold in the fresh coriander, ensuring everything is well mixed.
8. Season with additional salt and black pepper if desired and serve immediately or refrigerate for a chilled option.

NUTRITION FACTS PER 100G:
Energy: 137 kcal | Protein: 4g | Total Fat: 7g | Saturated Fat: 2g
Carbohydrates: 15g | Sugars: 2g | Dietary Fibre: 1g

Air Fryer Falafel Wraps with Tahini

SERVINGS: 4 | DIFFICULTY: MEDIUM | TEMPERATURE: 180°C
PREPARATION TIME: 15 MINUTES | COOKING TIME: 15 MINUTES

Ingredients:

* 400g canned chickpeas, drained and rinsed
* 1 small onion, finely chopped
* 2 cloves garlic, minced
* 15g fresh coriander, chopped
* 15g fresh parsley, chopped
* 1 tsp ground cumin
* 1 tsp ground coriander
* 1 tbsp flour
* salt and pepper to taste
* 1 tbsp olive oil
* 4 wholemeal wraps
* 100g fresh lettuce, shredded
* 1 tomato, sliced
* 1 cucumber, sliced
* 100g tahini sauce
* 1 lemon, cut into wedges

Preparation:

1. Begin by adding chickpeas, onion, garlic, fresh coriander, parsley, cumin, and ground coriander into a food processor. Blend until the mixture is coarse.
2. Incorporate flour, and season with salt and pepper. Pulse again until the mixture is just combined.
3. Shape the mixture into small balls or patties, approximately 18g each.
4. Lightly brush the falafel with olive oil on all sides.
5. Configure the air fryer to 180°C and preheat for 3 minutes.
6. Place falafel in the air fryer basket in a single layer, ensuring they are not touching.
7. Cook for 12 to 15 minutes, turning them halfway through the cooking time for even browning.
8. While falafel is cooking, prepare the wraps by laying them flat and placing a handful of the shredded lettuce in the centre.
9. Arrange slices of tomato and cucumber on top of the lettuce.
10. Once falafel is crunchy and golden brown, remove from air fryer and add to the wraps.
11. Drizzle with tahini sauce and squeeze a lemon wedge over each wrap.
12. Fold the wraps neatly and serve immediately.

***
NUTRITION FACTS PER 100G:
Energy: 178 kcal | Protein: 5g | Total Fat: 8g | Saturated Fat: 1g
Carbohydrates: 22g | Sugars: 2g | Dietary Fibre: 6g
***

Tuna Nicoise Salad with New Potatoes

SERVINGS: 4 | DIFFICULTY: MEDIUM | TEMPERATURE: 200°C
PREPARATION TIME: 15 MINUTES | COOKING TIME: 20 MINUTES

Ingredients:

* 400g new potatoes, halved
* 200g green beans, trimmed
* 2 tbsp olive oil
* 4 eggs
* 2 tuna steaks (approximately 200g each)
* 150g cherry tomatoes, halved
* 100g mixed salad leaves
* 10 black olives, pitted
* 2 tbsp lemon juice
* salt and pepper to taste

Preparation:

1. Start by preheating your air fryer to 200°C.
2. Toss the halved new potatoes with 1 tablespoon of olive oil, salt, and pepper. Place them in the air fryer basket and cook for 15 minutes, shaking halfway through.
3. As the potatoes are cooking, bring a pot of water to a boil and cook the eggs for 7 minutes. Cool them under cold running water, peel, and set aside.
4. Add the green beans to the air fryer with the potatoes for the final 5 minutes of cooking time.
5. Once the potatoes and green beans are done, remove them from the air fryer and let them cool slightly.
6. Drizzle the remaining olive oil over the tuna steaks and season with salt and pepper. Then, air fry the tuna steaks at 200°C for 6-8 minutes, turning midway through, to your preferred doneness.
7. Assemble the salad by arranging the salad leaves, cherry tomatoes, and olives on a large serving platter.
8. Scatter the cooked potatoes and green beans over the salad base.
9. Slice the eggs into quarters and add them to the salad.
10. Flake the cooked tuna over the top and finish with a drizzle of lemon juice before serving. Adjust seasoning if necessary.

NUTRITION FACTS PER 100G:
Energy: 135 kcal | Protein: 10g | Total Fat: 8g | Saturated Fat: 2g
Carbohydrates: 7g | Sugars: 2g | Dietary Fibre: 2g

Grilled Chicken Caesar Wraps

SERVINGS: 4 | DIFFICULTY: MEDIUM | TEMPERATURE: 180°C
PREPARATION TIME: 20 MINUTES | COOKING TIME: 20 MINUTES

Ingredients:

* 500g chicken breast, boneless and skinless
* 2 tbsp olive oil
* 1 tsp garlic powder
* 1 tsp paprika
* 1 tsp salt
* 1/2 tsp black pepper
* 4 large wholemeal wraps
* 100g romaine lettuce, roughly chopped
* 50g grated Parmesan cheese
* 120ml Caesar dressing
* 1 medium tomato, diced
* 1/2 small red onion, finely sliced

Preparation:

1. Preheat the air fryer to 180°C.
2. Cut the chicken breast into thin strips and place in a bowl.
3. Stir in olive oil, garlic powder, paprika, salt, and black pepper, ensuring the chicken is well coated.
4. Arrange the chicken strips in the air fryer basket. Cook for about 15-18 minutes, flipping halfway through until golden and cooked through.
5. Warm the wholemeal wraps in the air fryer for 1-2 minutes to make them pliable.
6. Assemble the wraps by layering romaine lettuce, cooked chicken, grated Parmesan, diced tomato, and red onion onto each wrap.
7. Drizzle Caesar dressing over the fillings.
8. Tightly roll the wraps, folding in the sides to secure the ingredients.
9. Serve immediately for a deliciously satisfying meal.

NUTRITION FACTS PER 100G:
Energy: 212 kcal | Protein: 15g | Total Fat: 11g | Saturated Fat: 3g
Carbohydrates: 14g | Sugars: 2g | Dietary Fibre: 1g

Beetroot and Goat's Cheese Salad

SERVINGS: 4 | DIFFICULTY: EASY | TEMPERATURE: 180°C
PREPARATION TIME: 10 MINUTES | COOKING TIME: 20 MINUTES

Ingredients:

* 500g beetroot, peeled and cut into wedges
* 2 tbsp olive oil
* 100g goat's cheese, crumbled
* 50g walnuts, roughly chopped
* 100g mixed salad leaves
* 2 tbsp balsamic glaze
* salt and pepper, to taste

Preparation:

1. Preheat the air fryer to 180°C.
2. In a mixing bowl, coat the beetroot wedges with olive oil, salt, and pepper.
3. Place the beetroot in the air fryer basket and cook for 20 minutes, shaking the basket halfway through.
4. In the meantime, arrange the mixed salad leaves on a serving platter.
5. Once cooked, allow the beetroot to cool slightly, then distribute it evenly over the salad leaves.
6. Sprinkle the crumbled goat's cheese and walnuts over the beetroot and leaves.
7. Drizzle the balsamic glaze across the salad just before serving.

NUTRITION FACTS PER 100G:
Energy: 143 kcal | Protein: 4g | Total Fat: 10g | Saturated Fat: 3g
Carbohydrates: 8g | Sugars: 5g | Dietary Fibre: 2g

Smoked Mackerel and Cucumber Salad

SERVINGS: 2 | DIFFICULTY: EASY | TEMPERATURE: 180°C
PREPARATION TIME: 15 MINUTES | COOKING TIME: 8 MINUTES

Ingredients:

* 150g smoked mackerel fillets
* 1 medium cucumber
* 2 tbsp Greek yoghurt
* 1 tbsp lemon juice
* 1 tbsp olive oil
* 1 tbsp fresh dill, chopped
* salt and pepper, to taste
* 50g mixed salad leaves
* 20g walnuts, roughly chopped

Preparation:

1. Preheat the air fryer to 180°C.
2. Slice the cucumber thinly and place in a mixing bowl.
3. Add Greek yoghurt, lemon juice, olive oil, and fresh dill to the bowl, seasoning with salt and pepper.
4. Stir the mixture until the cucumber is well coated.
5. Place the smoked mackerel fillets in the air fryer basket, cooking for 8 minutes until heated through.
6. Arrange mixed salad leaves on a serving plate.
7. Once the mackerel is ready, flake it gently with a fork and add it to the salad leaves.
8. Top the salad with the dressed cucumber and scatter chopped walnuts over.
9. Serve the salad immediately, drizzling extra lemon juice if desired.

NUTRITION FACTS PER 100G:
Energy: 173 kcal | Protein: 9g | Total Fat: 14g | Saturated Fat: 3g
Carbohydrates: 3g | Sugars: 2g | Dietary Fibre: 1g

Roast Veggie and Feta Couscous

SERVINGS: 4 | DIFFICULTY: EASY | TEMPERATURE: 200°C
PREPARATION TIME: 15 MINUTES | COOKING TIME: 20 MINUTES

Ingredients:

* 200g couscous
* 1 red pepper, diced
* 1 yellow pepper, diced
* 1 aubergine, diced
* 1 courgette, diced
* 2 tbsp olive oil
* 100g feta cheese, crumbled
* 2 tbsp fresh mint, chopped
* 2 tbsp fresh parsley, chopped
* 1 lemon, juiced
* 1 tsp salt
* 1/2 tsp black pepper

Preparation:

1. Preheat your air fryer to 200°C.
2. In a large bowl, combine the diced red pepper, yellow pepper, aubergine, and courgette. Drizzle with olive oil and mix well to ensure all pieces are coated.
3. Transfer the vegetable mixture to the air fryer basket and cook for 15 minutes, shaking the basket halfway through to ensure even roasting.
4. In the meantime, prepare the couscous according to the package instructions, usually involving boiling water, covering, and letting it sit for a few minutes.
5. Once the vegetables are roasted, remove them from the air fryer and allow them to cool slightly.
6. Fluff the cooked couscous with a fork and transfer it to a serving bowl.
7. Gently fold the roasted vegetables into the couscous.
8. Add the crumbled feta cheese, chopped mint, and parsley to the bowl. Toss to combine.
9. Drizzle the lemon juice over the mixture, and season with salt and black pepper according to taste.
10. Serve immediately, or refrigerate for an hour if you prefer a cold salad.

NUTRITION FACTS PER 100G:
- Energy: 120 kcal | - Protein: 3g | - Total Fat: 7g | - Saturated Fat: 2g
| - Carbohydrates: 13g | - Sugars: 3g | - Dietary Fibre: 2g

Poached Salmon and Watercress Sandwiches

SERVINGS: 4 | DIFFICULTY: MEDIUM | TEMPERATURE: 180°C
PREPARATION TIME: 15 MINUTES | COOKING TIME: 12 MINUTES

Ingredients:

* 4 salmon fillets (about 150g each)
* 150g watercress
* 8 slices of wholemeal bread
* 100ml Greek yoghurt
* 1 lemon, zested and juiced
* 1 tbsp olive oil
* salt, to taste
* black pepper, freshly ground, to taste

Preparation:

1. First, season the salmon fillets with salt and black pepper.
2. Mix the Greek yoghurt with lemon juice and zest in a small bowl.
3. Preheat the air fryer to 180°C.
4. Lay the seasoned salmon fillets in the air fryer basket, ensuring they're not overcrowded.
5. Cook the salmon for 10 minutes or until just cooked through.
6. Meanwhile, drizzle olive oil over the wholemeal bread slices.
7. Toast the bread slices in a separate device or in the air fryer if there's space.
8. Once the salmon is done, carefully flake it with a fork.
9. Spread the yoghurt mixture over the toasted bread slices.
10. Arrange a generous handful of watercress on four of the bread slices.
11. Top the watercress with the flaked salmon.
12. Cover with the remaining bread slices and gently press to form sandwiches.
13. Finally, halve the sandwiches diagonally and serve immediately.

NUTRITION FACTS PER 100G:
Energy: 190 kcal | Protein: 16g | Total Fat: 9g | Saturated Fat: 2g
Carbohydrates: 12g | Sugars: 2g | Dietary Fibre: 1g

Air Fryer Chickpea and Sweet Potato Patties

SERVINGS: 4 | DIFFICULTY: MEDIUM | TEMPERATURE: 200°C
PREPARATION TIME: 20 MINUTES | COOKING TIME: 18 MINUTES

Ingredients:

* 400g canned chickpeas, drained and rinsed
* 250g sweet potatoes, peeled and grated
* 1 small red onion, finely chopped
* 2 garlic cloves, minced
* 2 tbsp chopped fresh coriander
* 1 tsp ground cumin
* 1/2 tsp smoked paprika
* salt and pepper, to taste
* 50g breadcrumbs
* 2 tbsp olive oil
* 1 tbsp lemon juice

Preparation:

1. Start by placing the chickpeas in a large bowl. Use a potato masher or fork to slightly mash them, leaving some whole for texture.
2. Incorporate the grated sweet potatoes, chopped onion, and minced garlic into the mashed chickpeas. Mix well to combine.
3. Add the chopped coriander, ground cumin, smoked paprika, salt, and pepper into the chickpea mixture. Stir thoroughly.
4. Sprinkle the breadcrumbs over the mixture, followed by the olive oil and lemon juice. Mix until everything is well combined.
5. Shape the mixture into 8 equal-sized patties, pressing them firmly to ensure they hold together.
6. Preheat the air fryer to 200°C for a couple of minutes.
7. Arrange the patties in the air fryer basket in a single layer, making sure not to overcrowd them. You may need to cook in batches.
8. Cook the patties for 9 minutes, then flip them over and cook for an additional 9 minutes, or until they're golden brown and crispy on the outside.
9. Once cooked, remove the patties from the air fryer and let them rest for a few minutes before serving. Serve with your favourite sauce or salad.

NUTRITION FACTS PER 100G:
Energy: 141 kcal | Protein: 4g | Total Fat: 5g | Saturated Fat: 1g
Carbohydrates: 18g | Sugars: 3g | Dietary Fibre: 4g

Mediterranean Stuffed Peppers

SERVINGS: 4 | DIFFICULTY: MEDIUM | TEMPERATURE: 180°C
PREPARATION TIME: 15 MINUTES | COOKING TIME: 20 MINUTES

Ingredients:

* 4 large bell peppers
* 200g cooked quinoa
* 100g feta cheese, crumbled
* 50g black olives, sliced
* 50g sun-dried tomatoes, chopped
* 1 small red onion, finely chopped
* 2 tbsp olive oil
* 1 tbsp lemon juice
* 1 tsp dried oregano
* salt and pepper to taste
* fresh parsley, chopped, for garnish

Preparation:

1. Begin by preheating your air fryer to 180°C.
2. Meanwhile, slice the tops off the bell peppers and remove seeds and membranes.
3. Next, in a mixing bowl, combine cooked quinoa, feta cheese, black olives, sun-dried tomatoes, red onion, olive oil, lemon juice, dried oregano, salt and pepper.
4. Stuff the prepared mixture into each bell pepper generously.
5. Carefully place the stuffed peppers into the air fryer basket.
6. Cook in the preheated air fryer for 18-20 minutes until the peppers are tender and the tops start to brown.
7. Once cooked, remove from the air fryer and let them cool slightly.
8. Finally, garnish with fresh parsley before serving.

NUTRITION FACTS PER 100G:
Energy: 124 kcal | Protein: 4g | Total Fat: 8g | Saturated Fat: 2g
Carbohydrates: 10g | Sugars: 3g | Dietary Fibre: 3g

Grilled Asparagus and Poached Egg Salad

SERVINGS: 2 | DIFFICULTY: EASY | TEMPERATURE: 200°C
PREPARATION TIME: 10 MINUTES | COOKING TIME: 15 MINUTES

Ingredients:

* 200g asparagus, trimmed
* 2 large eggs
* 1 tbsp olive oil
* salt and pepper, to taste
* 1 tbsp white vinegar
* 50g mixed salad leaves
* 10 cherry tomatoes, halved
* 30g grated Parmesan cheese
* 1 tbsp lemon juice

Preparation:

1. Start by preheating the air fryer to 200°C.
2. Drizzle the asparagus with olive oil, then season generously with salt and pepper.
3. Arrange the seasoned asparagus in the air fryer basket and cook for 7-8 minutes until tender.
4. Meanwhile, bring a pot of water to a simmer and add the white vinegar.
5. Crack eggs individually into small bowls, then gently slide them into the simmering water.
6. Poach each egg for 3-4 minutes until the whites are set but the yolks remain runny.
7. Remove the asparagus from the air fryer and let it cool slightly.
8. In a large salad bowl, combine the mixed salad leaves, cherry tomatoes, and grilled asparagus.
9. Top the salad with the poached eggs and sprinkle with grated Parmesan cheese.
10. Finish with a squeeze of lemon juice over the salad before serving.

NUTRITION FACTS PER 100G:
Energy: 117 kcal | Protein: 7g | Total Fat: 9g | Saturated Fat: 2g
Carbohydrates: 2g | Sugars: 2g | Dietary Fibre: 1g

Avocado, Tomato and Mozzarella Salad

SERVINGS: 4 | DIFFICULTY: EASY | TEMPERATURE: 200°C
PREPARATION TIME: 10 MINUTES | COOKING TIME: 5 MINUTES

Ingredients:

* 2 ripe avocados, diced
* 200g cherry tomatoes, halved
* 250g mozzarella balls, drained
* 2 tbsp olive oil
* 1 tbsp balsamic vinegar
* salt and pepper to taste
* a handful of fresh basil leaves
* 1 tbsp pine nuts

Preparation:

1. Preheat the air fryer to 200°C.
2. In a large bowl, combine the diced avocados, halved cherry tomatoes, and mozzarella balls.
3. Drizzle olive oil and balsamic vinegar over the salad mixture, and season with salt and pepper. Toss gently to coat.
4. Transfer the salad mixture into the air fryer basket. Cook for 5 minutes, shaking halfway through.
5. Meanwhile, toast the pine nuts in a small pan over medium heat until golden brown.
6. Once finished, remove the salad mixture from the air fryer and place it in a serving dish.
7. Garnish with toasted pine nuts and fresh basil leaves before serving.

NUTRITION FACTS PER 100G:
Energy: 192 kcal | Protein: 6g | Total Fat: 16g | Saturated Fat: 5g
Carbohydrates: 5g | Sugars: 2g | Dietary Fibre: 3g

Air Fryer Lemon and Herb Chicken Skewers

SERVINGS: 4 | DIFFICULTY: EASY | TEMPERATURE: 200°C
PREPARATION TIME: 20 MINUTES | COOKING TIME: 15 MINUTES

Ingredients:

* 500g chicken breast, cut into cubes
* 1 lemon, juiced and zested
* 2 tbsp olive oil
* 2 tbsp fresh parsley, finely chopped
* 1 tbsp fresh thyme leaves
* 1 tsp garlic granules
* salt and pepper, to taste
* 1 red bell pepper, cut into squares
* 1 yellow bell pepper, cut into squares
* metal or wooden skewers (if wooden, soak them in water for 30 minutes prior to use)

Preparation:

1. Begin by creating the marinade. In a large bowl, combine the lemon juice and zest with olive oil, parsley, thyme, garlic granules, salt, and pepper.
2. Add the chicken cubes to the marinade, ensuring they are well-coated. Allow them to marinate for at least 15 minutes, or longer if you have time.
3. Meanwhile, prepare the skewers by alternating pieces of marinated chicken with chunks of red and yellow bell pepper.
4. Preheat the air fryer to 200°C.
5. Once preheated, place the skewers in a single layer inside the air fryer basket. Cook for 15 minutes, turning halfway through, until the chicken is cooked through and slightly charred.
6. Remove from the air fryer and let them rest for a couple of minutes before serving. Serve hot, garnished with extra parsley if desired.

NUTRITION FACTS PER 100G:
Energy: 148 kcal | Protein: 18 g | Total Fat: 8 g | Saturated Fat: 1 g
Carbohydrates: 3 g | Sugars: 2 g | Dietary Fibre: 1 g

Spinach and Ricotta Stuffed Mushrooms

SERVINGS: 4 | DIFFICULTY: EASY | TEMPERATURE: 190°C
PREPARATION TIME: 15 MINUTES | COOKING TIME: 12 MINUTES

Ingredients:

* 12 large button mushrooms, stems removed
* 200g fresh spinach leaves
* 150g ricotta cheese
* 50g grated Parmesan cheese
* 1 small garlic clove, minced
* 1 tbsp olive oil
* 1/2 tsp salt
* 1/4 tsp black pepper
* 1/4 tsp nutmeg
* 1 tbsp breadcrumbs
* 1 tbsp chopped fresh parsley

Preparation:

1. Preheat the air fryer to 190°C.
2. In a pan, heat olive oil over medium heat and sauté garlic until fragrant.
3. Add spinach to the pan and cook until wilted, then drain excess moisture.
4. Combine ricotta cheese, Parmesan, salt, pepper, and nutmeg in a bowl.
5. Chop the cooked spinach and mix it with the ricotta mixture.
6. Stuff each mushroom cap generously with the spinach and ricotta filling.
7. Sprinkle breadcrumbs evenly over the stuffed mushrooms.
8. Arrange the mushrooms in the air fryer basket in a single layer.
9. Cook for 12 minutes, or until the mushrooms are tender and the tops are golden brown.
10. Garnish with chopped parsley before serving.

NUTRITION FACTS PER 100G:
Energy: 136 kcal | Protein: 8g | Total Fat: 9g | Saturated Fat: 4g
Carbohydrates: 5g | Sugars: 2g | Dietary Fibre: 2g

Grilled Courgette and Red Pepper Paninis

SERVINGS: 2 | DIFFICULTY: EASY | TEMPERATURE: 200°C
PREPARATION TIME: 10 MINUTES | COOKING TIME: 8 MINUTES

Ingredients:

* 1 courgette, thinly sliced
* 1 red pepper, thinly sliced
* 1 tbsp olive oil
* salt and pepper to taste
* 100g mozzarella cheese, sliced
* 4 slices of ciabatta bread
* 2 tbsp pesto
* handful of fresh basil leaves

Preparation:

1. Begin by preheating your air fryer to 200°C.
2. Toss the courgette and red pepper slices in a bowl with olive oil, salt, and pepper, ensuring they are well coated.
3. Place the courgette and red pepper slices in the air fryer basket. Cook them for 5 minutes or until they are tender and lightly charred.
4. While the vegetables are cooking, spread pesto evenly on one side of each ciabatta slice.
5. Once the vegetables are ready, layer the grilled courgette, red pepper, and mozzarella cheese on two of the ciabatta slices.
6. Add fresh basil leaves on top of the cheese layer.
7. Top with the remaining ciabatta slices, pesto side down, to form the paninis.
8. Carefully place the assembled paninis in the air fryer basket.
9. Cook for an additional 3 minutes or until the cheese is melted and the bread is golden brown.
10. Serve warm and enjoy your delicious air-fried paninis.

NUTRITION FACTS PER 100G:
Energy: 226 kcal | Protein: 9g | Total Fat: 14g | Saturated Fat: 5g
Carbohydrates: 17g | Sugars: 2g | Dietary Fibre: 3g

Pear, Walnut, and Stilton Salad

SERVINGS: 4 | DIFFICULTY: EASY | TEMPERATURE: 180°C
PREPARATION TIME: 15 MINUTES | COOKING TIME: 10 MINUTES

Ingredients:

* 2 pears, cored and sliced
* 100g walnuts
* 100g Stilton cheese, crumbled
* 100g mixed salad leaves
* 2 tbsp olive oil
* 1 tbsp balsamic vinegar
* salt and pepper, to taste

Preparation:

1. Preheat the air fryer to 180°C.
2. Toss the walnut halves in a tablespoon of olive oil, ensuring they are well coated.
3. Place the walnuts in the air fryer basket and cook for 5 minutes, shaking halfway through.
4. Arrange the sliced pears and mixed salad leaves in a large salad bowl.
5. Once the walnuts are done, allow them to cool slightly before adding to the salad.
6. Sprinkle the crumbled Stilton over the salad.
7. In a small bowl, whisk together the remaining olive oil, balsamic vinegar, salt, and pepper to create the dressing.
8. Drizzle the dressing over the salad just before serving and gently toss to combine.

NUTRITION FACTS PER 100G:
Energy: 230 kcal | Protein: 5g | Total Fat: 20g | Saturated Fat: 4g
Carbohydrates: 9g | Sugars: 5g | Dietary Fibre: 2g

Chapter 4:
Fish and Seafood Delights

Air Fryer Fish and Chips with Mushy Peas

SERVINGS: 4 | DIFFICULTY: MEDIUM | TEMPERATURE: 200°C
PREPARATION TIME: 15 MINUTES | COOKING TIME: 30 MINUTES

Ingredients:

* 600g white fish fillets (cod or haddock)
* 500g potatoes, cut into chips
* 100g plain flour
* 1 tsp baking powder
* 150ml cold sparkling water
* 1 egg
* salt and pepper, to taste
* 200g frozen peas
* 1 tbsp mint, chopped
* 1 tbsp butter
* 1 lemon, cut into wedges
* cooking oil spray

Preparation:

1. Begin by preheating the air fryer to 200°C.
2. Season the potato chips with salt and pepper, then spray lightly with cooking oil.
3. Place the chips in the air fryer basket and cook for 15 minutes, shaking halfway through.
4. In a bowl, mix flour, baking powder, a pinch of salt, and some pepper.
5. Crack the egg into the mixture and add sparkling water gradually, whisking to form a batter.
6. Dip each fish fillet in the batter, ensuring an even coating.
7. Remove the chips from the air fryer and set aside, keeping them warm.
8. Next, place the battered fish in the air fryer, cooking for 10-12 minutes until golden and crispy.
9. For the mushy peas, cook peas in boiling water for 3-4 minutes, then drain.
10. Mash the peas roughly, stirring in butter and mint, seasoning with salt and pepper.
11. Finally, serve the fish and chips with mushy peas on the side and garnish with lemon wedges.

NUTRITION FACTS PER 100G:
Energy: 180 kcal | Protein: 12g | Total Fat: 7g | Saturated Fat: 1g
Carbohydrates: 20g | Sugars: 1g | Dietary Fibre: 2g

Crispy Battered Prawns with Sweet Chilli Dip

SERVINGS: 4 | DIFFICULTY: MEDIUM | TEMPERATURE: 200°C
PREPARATION TIME: 15 MINUTES | COOKING TIME: 10 MINUTES

Ingredients:

* 500g large prawns, peeled and deveined
* 100g plain flour
* 100ml cold sparkling water
* 1 egg
* 1/2 tsp baking powder
* 1 pinch of salt
* 1 pinch of black pepper
* Vegetable oil spray
* 100ml sweet chilli sauce
* fresh coriander leaves for garnish

Preparation:

1. Begin by whisking the plain flour, cold sparkling water, egg, baking powder, salt, and black pepper in a bowl until the batter is smooth.
2. Dip each prawn into the batter, ensuring they are completely coated.
3. Preheat the air fryer to 200°C.
4. Place the battered prawns in the air fryer basket in a single layer, taking care not to overcrowd.
5. Lightly spray the prawns with a vegetable oil spray to assist in crisping.
6. Cook the prawns for 10 minutes, turning them halfway through the cooking time to ensure even browning.
7. Warm the sweet chilli sauce separately and serve alongside the crispy prawns.
8. Garnish with fresh coriander leaves for a burst of colour and additional flavour before serving.

NUTRITION FACTS PER 100G:
Energy: 165 kcal | Protein: 10g | Total Fat: 5g | Saturated Fat: 1g
Carbohydrates: 22g | Sugars: 4g | Dietary Fibre: 1g

Grilled Mackerel with Lemon and Thyme

SERVINGS: 2 | DIFFICULTY: EASY | TEMPERATURE: 180°C
PREPARATION TIME: 10 MINUTES | COOKING TIME: 20 MINUTES

Ingredients:

* 2 fresh mackerel fillets (approximately 200geach)
* 1 tbsp olive oil
* 1 lemon, sliced thinly
* 3 sprigs of fresh thyme
* salt, to taste
* black pepper, to taste
* 1 clove garlic, finely chopped

Preparation:

1. Begin by preheating your air fryer to 180°C.
2. Next, pat the mackerel fillets dry with kitchen paper and place them on a plate.
3. Drizzle the olive oil over the fillets, ensuring both sides are coated evenly.
4. Season the mackerel generously with salt and black pepper.
5. Spread the chopped garlic over the fillets and top each fillet with lemon slices.
6. Place the fresh thyme sprigs over the lemon-topped fillets.
7. Gently place the prepared mackerel fillets in the air fryer basket.
8. Cook the mackerel for 20 minutes until the skin is crispy and the fish is cooked through.
9. Once done, carefully remove from the air fryer and serve immediately.

NUTRITION FACTS PER 100G:
Energy: 219 kcal | Protein: 19g | Total Fat: 16g | Saturated Fat: 3g
Carbohydrates: 1g | Sugars: 0g | Dietary Fibre: 1g

Smoked Haddock Fishcakes with a Crispy Coating

SERVINGS: 4 | DIFFICULTY: MEDIUM | TEMPERATURE: 200°C
PREPARATION TIME: 20 MINUTES | COOKING TIME: 15 MINUTES

Ingredients:

* 300g smoked haddock fillets, poached and flaked
* 200g potatoes, peeled and boiled
* 1 tbsp butter
* 2 tbsp chopped fresh parsley
* 1 lemon, zested
* salt and pepper, to taste
* 100g plain flour
* 1 egg, beaten
* 100g breadcrumbs
* olive oil spray

Preparation:

1. Begin by mashing the boiled potatoes with the butter in a large bowl until smooth.
2. Add the flaked smoked haddock, chopped parsley, lemon zest, salt, and pepper to the mashed potatoes. Mix well to combine all ingredients evenly.
3. Shape the haddock mixture into 8 equally sized cakes.
4. Prepare three separate plates for coating: one with plain flour, the second with beaten egg, and the third with breadcrumbs.
5. Dredge each fishcake first in the flour, shaking off any excess, then dip into the beaten egg, and finally coat in breadcrumbs.
6. Arrange the coated fishcakes onto a plate and lightly spray them with olive oil.
7. Preheat the air fryer to 200°C.
8. Carefully place the fishcakes in the air fryer basket in a single layer, ensuring they do not touch.
9. Cook for 15 minutes, flipping halfway through, until the fishcakes are golden and crispy.
10. Serve immediately with your favourite accompaniment.

NUTRITION FACTS PER 100G:
Energy: 150 kcal | Protein: 8g | Total Fat: 4g | Saturated Fat: 1g
Carbohydrates: 18g | Sugars: 1g | Dietary Fibre: 1g

Breaded Sole Fillets with Tartar Sauce

SERVINGS: 4 | DIFFICULTY: EASY | TEMPERATURE: 200°C
PREPARATION TIME: 15 MINUTES | COOKING TIME: 12 MINUTES

Ingredients:

* 4 sole fillets (about 120g each)
* 100g breadcrumbs
* 50g plain flour
* 2 eggs
* 1 tsp salt
* 1/2 tsp black pepper
* 1/2 tsp garlic powder
* 1/2 tsp paprika
* 2 tbsp olive oil
* lemon wedges, for serving
* 200ml mayonnaise
* 2 tbsp chopped gherkins
* 1 tbsp capers, chopped
* 1 tbsp freshly chopped parsley
* 1 tbsp lemon juice
* 1/2 tsp Dijon mustard

Preparation:

1. Begin by preheating the air fryer to 200°C.
2. Set out three shallow bowls: one with plain flour, another with beaten eggs, and a third with a mixture of breadcrumbs, salt, black pepper, garlic powder, and paprika.
3. Dip each sole fillet first into the flour, ensuring it's fully coated.
4. Next, immerse the flour-coated fillet in the beaten eggs, allowing the excess to drip off.
5. Finally, press the fillet into the breadcrumb mixture, making sure it's evenly covered.
6. Lightly brush the olive oil over both sides of the breaded fillets.
7. Place the fillets in the air fryer basket in a single layer, working in batches if necessary.
8. Cook for 6 minutes, then flip the fillets and continue to cook for another 6 minutes until golden brown and crispy.
9. While the fish is cooking, prepare the tartar sauce by combining the mayonnaise, chopped gherkins, capers, parsley, lemon juice, and Dijon mustard in a bowl.
10. Serve the crispy sole fillets with lemon wedges and a generous dollop of tartar sauce on the side.

NUTRITION FACTS PER 100G:
Energy: 230 kcal | Protein: 11g | Total Fat: 15g | Saturated Fat: 3g
Carbohydrates: 15g | Sugars: 1g | Dietary Fibre: 1g

Air Fryer Scallops with Garlic Butter

SERVINGS: 4 | DIFFICULTY: EASY | TEMPERATURE: 200°C
PREPARATION TIME: 10 MINUTES | COOKING TIME: 8 MINUTES

Ingredients:

* 16 large scallops (approximately 500g)
* 60g unsalted butter
* 4 garlic cloves, minced
* 2 tbsp fresh lemon juice
* 1 tbsp chopped fresh parsley
* 1/2 tsp sea salt
* 1/4 tsp freshly ground black pepper
* 1 tbsp olive oil

Preparation:

1. Begin by patting the scallops dry with a paper towel to remove excess moisture.
2. In a small saucepan, melt the butter over low heat. Once melted, stir in the minced garlic and cook for 1 minute until fragrant.
3. Add lemon juice to the butter mixture and stir well. Remove from heat and mix in the chopped parsley, salt, and pepper.
4. Preheat the air fryer to 200°C.
5. Lightly coat the scallops with olive oil and place them evenly in the air fryer basket, ensuring they are not touching.
6. Cook the scallops for 4 minutes. Using tongs, carefully flip them over and continue cooking for an additional 4 minutes.
7. Once cooked, drizzle the garlic butter sauce over the scallops immediately.
8. Serve the scallops hot, garnished with a little extra parsley if desired.

> **NUTRITION FACTS PER 100G:**
> Energy: 128 kcal | Protein: 12g | Total Fat: 8g | Saturated Fat: 4g
> Carbohydrates: 2g | Sugars: 1g | Dietary Fibre: 0g

Grilled Seabass with Herby Potatoes

SERVINGS: 2 | DIFFICULTY: MODERATE | TEMPERATURE: 200°C
PREPARATION TIME: 15 MINUTES | COOKING TIME: 25 MINUTES

Ingredients:

* 2 seabass fillets
* 300g baby potatoes
* 2 tbsp olive oil
* 1 lemon, sliced
* 2 cloves garlic, minced
* 1 tbsp fresh parsley, chopped
* 1 tbsp fresh dill, chopped
* 1 tsp sea salt
* 1 tsp black pepper
* 1 tsp paprika

Preparation:

1. Start by washing and halving the baby potatoes. Place them in a bowl and toss with 1 tablespoon of olive oil, minced garlic, parsley, dill, sea salt, and black pepper.
2. Preheat the air fryer to 200°C. Once ready, spread the herby potatoes evenly in the air fryer basket and cook for 15 minutes, shaking the basket halfway through.
3. Meanwhile, prepare the seabass fillets. Rub them with the remaining olive oil, and season with sea salt, black pepper, and paprika.
4. After 15 minutes, move the potatoes to one side of the air fryer basket and place the seasoned seabass fillets next to them. Lay lemon slices on top of each fillet.
5. Continue cooking for an additional 10 minutes at 200°C, until the seabass is fully cooked and the potatoes are crispy and golden.
6. Once done, carefully remove from the air fryer. Serve the grilled seabass with herby potatoes immediately for best flavour and texture.

> **NUTRITION FACTS PER 100G:**
> Energy: 118 kcal | Protein: 9g | Total Fat: 6g | Saturated Fat: 1g
> Carbohydrates: 11g | Sugars: 1g | Dietary Fibre: 2g

Prawn and Avocado Cocktail with a Twist

SERVINGS: 4 | DIFFICULTY: MEDIUM | TEMPERATURE: 200°C
PREPARATION TIME: 15 MINUTES | COOKING TIME: 10 MINUTES

Ingredients:

* 200g raw prawns, peeled and deveined
* 1 tbsp olive oil
* 1 tsp smoked paprika
* 1 avocado, diced
* 100g cherry tomatoes, halved
* 50g mixed salad greens
* 2 tbsp mayonnaise
* 1 tbsp lemon juice
* 1 tsp Worcestershire sauce
* salt and pepper to taste

Preparation:

1. Start by preheating the air fryer to 200°C.
2. In a bowl, combine prawns, olive oil, and smoked paprika. Ensure the prawns are coated evenly.
3. Transfer the prawns to the air fryer basket. Cook for 5-7 minutes until they turn pink and opaque.
4. Meanwhile, prepare the dressing by mixing mayonnaise, lemon juice, Worcestershire sauce, salt, and pepper in a small bowl.
5. In a large mixing bowl, combine diced avocado, cherry tomatoes, and mixed salad greens.
6. Add the cooked prawns to the salad mixture and gently toss to combine.
7. Drizzle the prepared dressing over the salad, ensuring even distribution.
8. Serve the prawn and avocado cocktail immediately, allowing the flavours to shine through.

NUTRITION FACTS PER 100G:
Energy: 180 kcal | Protein: 9g | Total Fat: 14g | Saturated Fat: 2g
Carbohydrates: 5g | Sugars: 1g | Dietary Fibre: 3g

Air Fryer Calamari with Lemon Aioli

SERVINGS: 4 | DIFFICULTY: MEDIUM | TEMPERATURE: 200°C
PREPARATION TIME: 15 MINUTES | COOKING TIME: 10 MINUTES

Ingredients:

* 500g calamari rings
* 100g plain flour
* 1 tsp salt
* 1 tsp black pepper
* 1 tsp garlic powder
* 1 tsp paprika
* 2 large eggs
* 150g breadcrumbs
* 100ml mayonnaise
* 1 tbsp lemon juice
* 1 garlic clove, minced
* 1 tbsp fresh parsley, chopped
* lemon wedges, for serving

Preparation:

1. Start by preparing the calamari. Rinse the calamari rings under cold water and pat them dry with a paper towel.
2. In a shallow bowl, combine the plain flour, salt, black pepper, garlic powder, and paprika. Mix thoroughly.
3. Break the eggs into another bowl and beat them until well combined.
4. Place the breadcrumbs in a third bowl, ready to coat the calamari.
5. Dredge each calamari ring in the flour mixture, shaking off the excess, then dip into the beaten eggs.
6. Coat the rings with breadcrumbs, ensuring each piece is well covered. Lay them on a plate.
7. Preheat the air fryer to 200°C for about 5 minutes.
8. Once preheated, arrange the calamari rings in the air fryer basket in a single layer.
9. Cook for 10 minutes or until golden brown and crispy, shaking the basket halfway through the cooking time.
10. Meanwhile, prepare the lemon aioli by stirring together the mayonnaise, lemon juice, minced garlic, and fresh parsley in a small bowl.
11. Serve the air-fried calamari with the lemon aioli and lemon wedges on the side.

NUTRITION FACTS PER 100G:
Energy: 220 kcal | Protein: 10g | Total Fat: 10g | Saturated Fat: 2g
Carbohydrates: 22g | Sugars: 1g | Dietary Fibre: 1g

Haddock and Leek Fish Pie

SERVINGS: 4 | DIFFICULTY: MODERATE | TEMPERATURE: 180°C
PREPARATION TIME: 20 MINUTES | COOKING TIME: 35 MINUTES

Ingredients:

* 400g haddock fillets
* 1 large leek, sliced
* 200g potatoes, peeled and cubed
* 75g butter
* 150ml milk
* 2 tbsp plain flour
* 100ml fish stock
* 100ml double cream
* 1 tbsp Dijon mustard
* 1 tbsp fresh parsley, chopped
* salt and pepper to taste
* 75g cheddar cheese, grated
* 1 tbsp olive oil

Preparation:

1. First, boil the potatoes in a pot of salted water until tender, about 12-15 minutes. Drain and set aside for later.
2. Meanwhile, heat the olive oil in a frying pan over medium heat. Add the sliced leek and sauté until soft, taking care not to brown them.
3. Melt 50g of the butter in a separate pan over low heat. Stir in the flour and cook for 1 minute, creating a paste.
4. Gradually whisk the milk and fish stock into the paste, continuing to stir until a smooth sauce forms.
5. Introduce the double cream, Dijon mustard, and season to taste with salt and pepper. Allow to simmer gently for a few minutes until the sauce thickens slightly.
6. Add the haddock fillets and poach in the sauce for 6-8 minutes until the fish is cooked through.
7. Stir in the cooked leeks, chopped parsley, and check the seasoning.
8. Preheat the air fryer to 180°C.
9. Place the fish and leek mixture in an air fryer-friendly baking dish.
10. Mash the cooked potatoes with the remaining 25g butter and season with salt and pepper to taste.
11. Spread the mashed potato evenly over the fish mixture, then sprinkle the grated cheddar cheese on top.
12. Insert the dish into the air fryer and cook for 20-25 minutes, or until the pie is heated through and the cheese is golden brown.
13. Carefully remove from the air fryer, allow to cool for a few minutes before serving.

NUTRITION FACTS PER 100G:
Energy: 155 kcal | Protein: 9g | Total Fat: 12g | Saturated Fat: 7g
Carbohydrates: 7g | Sugars: 1g | Dietary Fibre: 1g

Air Fryer Salmon with Dill and Lemon

SERVINGS: 2 | DIFFICULTY: EASY | TEMPERATURE: 180°C
PREPARATION TIME: 10 MINUTES | COOKING TIME: 12 MINUTES

Ingredients:

* 2 salmon fillets (approx. 150g each)
* 1 tbsp olive oil
* 1 tbsp fresh dill, chopped
* 1 lemon, sliced
* salt, to taste
* black pepper, to taste

Preparation:

1. Begin by patting the salmon fillets dry with kitchen paper.
2. Brush each fillet with olive oil on all sides.
3. Sprinkle dill evenly over the salmon pieces.
4. Season the fillets with salt and black pepper to your preference.
5. Lay lemon slices on top of each salmon fillet.
6. Preheat your air fryer to 180°C for 3 minutes.
7. Place the seasoned fillets in the air fryer basket.
8. Cook for 12 minutes or until the salmon is cooked through and flakes easily.
9. Carefully remove the salmon and serve with additional lemon slices, if desired.

NUTRITION FACTS PER 100G:
Energy: 250 kcal | Protein: 22g | Total Fat: 18g | Saturated Fat: 3g
Carbohydrates: 1g | Sugars: 0g | Dietary Fibre: 0g

Crab Cakes with a Zesty Mayo

SERVINGS: 4 | DIFFICULTY: MEDIUM | TEMPERATURE: 200°C
PREPARATION TIME: 15 MINUTES | COOKING TIME: 12 MINUTES

Ingredients:

* 300g crab meat
* 70g breadcrumbs
* 2 tbsp mayonnaise
* 1 egg
* 1 tbsp Dijon mustard
* 1 tbsp Worcestershire sauce
* 1 tbsp lemon juice
* 1 tsp smoked paprika
* 1 tsp garlic powder
* salt and pepper, to taste

* 2 tbsp chopped fresh parsley
* cooking spray

Zesty Mayo:
* 100ml mayonnaise
* 1 tbsp lemon juice
* 1 tsp Dijon mustard
* 1 tsp hot sauce
* 1 tsp grated lemon zest

Preparation:

1. Begin by preheating your air fryer to 200°C.
2. In a large bowl, combine the crab meat, breadcrumbs, mayonnaise, egg, Dijon mustard, Worcestershire sauce, lemon juice, smoked paprika, garlic powder, salt, and pepper.
3. Stir in the chopped parsley until the mixture is evenly combined.
4. Shape the mixture into 8 equal-sized patties.
5. Lightly spray the air fryer basket with cooking spray.
6. Arrange the crab cakes in a single layer in the basket, making sure they do not touch.
7. Cook the crab cakes for 10-12 minutes, turning halfway through, until they are golden brown.
8. While the crab cakes are cooking, prepare the zesty mayo by mixing together mayonnaise, lemon juice, Dijon mustard, hot sauce, and lemon zest in a small bowl.
9. Once the crab cakes are done, remove them from the air fryer and serve immediately with the zesty mayo on the side.

NUTRITION FACTS PER 100G:
Energy: 196 kcal | Protein: 13g | Total Fat: 14g | Saturated Fat: 2g
Carbohydrates: 9g | Sugars: 1g | Dietary Fibre: 1g

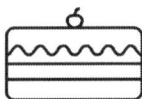

Grilled Tuna Steaks with a Soy and Ginger Marinade

SERVINGS: 2 | DIFFICULTY: EASY | TEMPERATURE: 200°C
PREPARATION TIME: 15 MINUTES | COOKING TIME: 8 MINUTES

Ingredients:

* 2 tuna steaks (approximately 150g each)
* 60ml soy sauce
* 1 tbsp fresh ginger, grated
* 1 tbsp honey
* 1 tbsp sesame oil
* 1 tsp garlic, minced
* 1 tsp freshly ground black pepper
* 1 tbsp sesame seeds
* 2 spring onions, finely chopped
* lemon wedges, to serve

Preparation:

1. Combine the soy sauce, grated ginger, honey, sesame oil, minced garlic, and black pepper in a small mixing bowl to create the marinade.
2. Place the tuna steaks into a shallow dish and pour the marinade over them, ensuring an even coating. Allow them to marinate for at least 15 minutes, turning halfway through.
3. Preheat the air fryer to 200°C.
4. Once preheated, carefully place the marinated tuna steaks into the air fryer basket.
5. Cook the steaks for approximately 4 minutes per side, or until desired doneness.
6. While the tuna is cooking, toast the sesame seeds in a dry pan over medium heat until golden.
7. Once cooking is complete, remove the tuna steaks and let them rest briefly.
8. Sprinkle with toasted sesame seeds and chopped spring onions, serving immediately alongside lemon wedges.

NUTRITION FACTS PER 100G:
Energy: 134 kcal | Protein: 20g | Total Fat: 5g | Saturated Fat: 1g
Carbohydrates: 5g | Sugars: 4g | Dietary Fibre: 1g

Crispy Whitebait with a Lemon Wedge

SERVINGS: 4 | DIFFICULTY: EASY | TEMPERATURE: 200°C
PREPARATION TIME: 10 MINUTES | COOKING TIME: 15 MINUTES

Ingredients:

* 400g whitebait
* 50g plain flour
* 1 tsp sea salt
* 1 tsp ground black pepper
* 1 tsp paprika
* 2 tbsp olive oil
* lemon wedges, for serving

Preparation:

1. Begin by rinsing the whitebait under cold water, then pat dry with kitchen towel.
2. In a large bowl, combine the plain flour, sea salt, ground black pepper, and paprika.
3. Coat the whitebait in the flour mixture, ensuring each fish is evenly covered.
4. Drizzle olive oil over the coated whitebait and toss gently to combine.
5. Preheat your air fryer to 200°C.
6. Once preheated, place the whitebait in the air fryer basket, spreading them in a single layer if possible.
7. Cook the whitebait for 15 minutes, shaking the basket halfway through to ensure even browning.
8. Serve the crispy whitebait hot, accompanied by fresh lemon wedges for squeezing over just before eating.

NUTRITION FACTS PER 100G:
Energy: 220 kcal | Protein: 16g | Total Fat: 15g | Saturated Fat: 3g
Carbohydrates: 8g | Sugars: 0g | Dietary Fibre: 1g

Air Fryer Cod with a Herb Crust

SERVINGS: 4 | DIFFICULTY: EASY | TEMPERATURE: 200°C
PREPARATION TIME: 10 MINUTES | COOKING TIME: 12 MINUTES

Ingredients:

* 4 cod fillets (about 150g each)
* 50g breadcrumbs
* 2 tbsp chopped fresh parsley
* 1 tbsp chopped fresh dill
* 1 tbsp chopped fresh chives
* 2 tbsp grated Parmesan cheese
* salt and pepper to taste
* 1 tbsp olive oil
* lemon wedges, for serving

Preparation:

1. Begin by preheating your air fryer to 200°C.
2. In a mixing bowl, combine the breadcrumbs, parsley, dill, chives, and Parmesan cheese.
3. Season the mixture with salt and pepper according to your taste preferences.
4. Drizzle the olive oil over the herb mixture and toss until evenly coated.
5. Arrange the cod fillets on a clean surface, then press the herb mixture firmly onto the top of each fillet.
6. Place the crusted cod fillets in the air fryer basket, making sure they are in a single layer.
7. Cook the fillets in the air fryer for approximately 12 minutes, or until the fish is cooked through and the crust is golden brown.
8. Serve the air-fried cod immediately with lemon wedges on the side.

NUTRITION FACTS PER 100G:
Energy: 150 kcal | Protein: 18g | Total Fat: 6g | Saturated Fat: 2g
Carbohydrates: 6g | Sugars: 1g | Dietary Fibre: 1g

Grilled Lobster Tails with Garlic Butter

SERVINGS: 4 | DIFFICULTY: MEDIUM | TEMPERATURE: 200°C
PREPARATION TIME: 15 MINUTES | COOKING TIME: 10 MINUTES

Ingredients:

* 4 lobster tails
* 100g unsalted butter
* 4 cloves garlic, minced
* 1 tbsp lemon juice
* 1 tbsp fresh parsley, chopped
* 1 tsp sea salt
* 1/2 tsp black pepper
* lemon wedges, for serving

Preparation:

1. Begin by pre-heating your air fryer to 200°C.
2. Cut the top of the lobster shells lengthwise using kitchen scissors, without cutting the meat, and gently pull the meat out to rest on top of the shell.
3. Season the lobster tails with sea salt and black pepper, ensuring an even coating.
4. In a small saucepan, melt the unsalted butter over medium heat.
5. Combine the minced garlic and lemon juice with the melted butter, stirring well.
6. Drizzle the garlic butter mixture generously over each lobster tail.
7. Arrange the lobster tails in the air fryer basket, spacing them evenly apart.
8. Cook in the air fryer for 8-10 minutes or until the meat is opaque and fork-tender.
9. Sprinkle fresh parsley over the cooked lobster tails for garnish.
10. Serve immediately with lemon wedges on the side.

NUTRITION FACTS PER 100G:
Energy: 180 kcal | Protein: 17g | Total Fat: 12g | Saturated Fat: 7g
Carbohydrates: 1g | Sugars: 0g | Dietary Fibre: 0g

Baked Sea Bream with Fennel and Lemon

SERVINGS: 2 | DIFFICULTY: EASY | TEMPERATURE: 180°C
PREPARATION TIME: 10 MINUTES | COOKING TIME: 20 MINUTES

Ingredients:

* 2 sea bream fillets (about 200g each)
* 1 small fennel bulb, thinly sliced
* 1 lemon, thinly sliced
* 2 tbsp olive oil
* 2 tsp fennel seeds
* salt, to taste
* black pepper, to taste
* a handful of fresh dill, chopped

Preparation:

1. Begin by preheating the air fryer to 180°C.
2. In a mixing bowl, combine the sliced fennel and lemon with olive oil, fennel seeds, salt, and pepper.
3. Lay a piece of foil in the air fryer basket, ensuring the edges are turned up to create a slight lip.
4. Place the fennel and lemon mixture onto the foil, spreading it out evenly.
5. Arrange the sea bream fillets on top of the fennel and lemon, skin side up.
6. Lightly drizzle olive oil over the fish, and season with additional salt and pepper.
7. Air fry for 20 minutes, or until the fish is cooked through and the skin is crispy.
8. Remove carefully from the air fryer, letting it rest for a minute.
9. Garnish with fresh dill before serving.

NUTRITION FACTS PER 100G:
Energy: 163 kcal | Protein: 16g | Total Fat: 11g | Saturated Fat: 2g
Carbohydrates: 2g | Sugars: 1g | Dietary Fibre: 1g

Plaice Goujons with Homemade Chips

SERVINGS: 4 | DIFFICULTY: EASY | TEMPERATURE: 200°C
PREPARATION TIME: 15 MINUTES | COOKING TIME: 25 MINUTES

Ingredients:

* 500g plaice fillets, skin removed and cut into strips
* 2 large potatoes, peeled and cut into chips
* 100g plain flour
* 2 eggs, beaten
* 100g breadcrumbs
* 1 tsp paprika
* salt and pepper to taste
* 2 tbsp vegetable oil
* lemon wedges, to serve

Preparation:

1. Start by preheating the air fryer to 200°C.
2. Prepare the potatoes by soaking them in cold water for about 10 minutes, then pat dry.
3. Toss the chips with 1 tbsp of vegetable oil and a pinch of salt, then arrange them in the air fryer basket.
4. Cook the chips for 15 minutes, shaking halfway through to ensure even cooking.
5. While the chips are cooking, set up a breading station with three plates: one with flour, one with beaten eggs, and one with breadcrumbs mixed with paprika, salt, and pepper.
6. Dredge each plaice strip in the flour, then dip into the egg, and finally coat with the breadcrumb mixture.
7. Lightly spray or brush the plaice goujons with the remaining vegetable oil.
8. Once the chips are par-cooked, move them to one side of the air fryer basket and place the goujons on the other side.
9. Continue cooking for another 10 minutes, or until the goujons are golden and the chips are crispy.
10. Finally, serve the plaice goujons and chips hot with lemon wedges on the side.

NUTRITION FACTS PER 100G:
Energy: 210 kcal | Protein: 13g | Total Fat: 8g | Saturated Fat: 1g
Carbohydrates: 25g | Sugars: 1g | Dietary Fibre: 2g

Prawn and Chorizo Skewers

SERVINGS: 4 | DIFFICULTY: EASY | TEMPERATURE: 200°C
PREPARATION TIME: 15 MINUTES | COOKING TIME: 10 MINUTES

Ingredients:

* 300g raw king prawns, peeled and deveined
* 150g chorizo, sliced
* 2 tbsp olive oil
* 1 tbsp lemon juice
* 2 garlic cloves, minced
* 1 tsp smoked paprika
* 1/2 tsp chilli flakes
* salt and pepper to taste
* fresh coriander, chopped (for garnish)
* lemon wedges (for serving)
* skewers

Preparation:

1. Begin by soaking the skewers in water for about 10 minutes to prevent them from burning.
2. In a bowl, mix together olive oil, lemon juice, minced garlic, smoked paprika, chilli flakes, salt, and pepper to create a marinade.
3. Combine prawns and chorizo slices in the marinade, ensuring they are thoroughly coated. Allow them to marinate for at least 10 minutes.
4. Thread the marinated prawns and chorizo alternately onto the skewers.
5. Place the skewers in the air fryer basket, making sure they are not overcrowded.
6. Set the air fryer to 200°C and cook the skewers for 8-10 minutes, turning them halfway through, until the prawns are pink and cooked through.
7. Garnish with fresh coriander and serve with lemon wedges for a burst of freshness.

NUTRITION FACTS PER 100G:
Energy: 180 kcal | Protein: 16g | Total Fat: 12g | Saturated Fat: 4g
Carbohydrates: 2g | Sugars: 1g | Dietary Fibre: 1g

Air Fryer Monkfish with Garlic and Parsley

SERVINGS: 2 | DIFFICULTY: MEDIUM | TEMPERATURE: 190°C
PREPARATION TIME: 10 MINUTES | COOKING TIME: 15 MINUTES

Ingredients:

* 400g monkfish tails
* 3 cloves garlic, minced
* 2 tbsp olive oil
* 1 tbsp lemon juice
* salt, to taste
* black pepper, to taste
* 2 tbsp fresh parsley, chopped
* lemon wedges, to serve

Preparation:

1. Begin by preheating your air fryer to 190°C.
2. In a small bowl, combine the minced garlic, olive oil, lemon juice, salt, and black pepper, creating a marinade.
3. Coat the monkfish tails evenly with the marinade, ensuring they are fully covered.
4. Place the marinated monkfish tails in the air fryer basket in a single layer for even cooking.
5. Cook the monkfish for about 15 minutes, turning halfway through for optimal results.
6. Once done, check to make sure the fish is opaque and flakes easily with a fork.
7. Serve immediately, garnishing with freshly chopped parsley and lemon wedges for an added zest.

NUTRITION FACTS PER 100G:
Energy: 155 kcal | Protein: 19g | Total Fat: 8g | Saturated Fat: 1g
Carbohydrates: 1g | Sugars: 0g | Dietary Fibre: 0g

Chapter 5:
Meat-Free Favourites

Stuffed Aubergines with Couscous and Feta

SERVINGS: 4 | DIFFICULTY: MEDIUM | TEMPERATURE: 180°C
PREPARATION TIME: 20 MINUTES | COOKING TIME: 30 MINUTES

Ingredients:

* 2 large aubergines
* 150g couscous
* 200ml vegetable stock
* 100g feta cheese, crumbled
* 1 red onion, finely chopped
* 1 red pepper, diced
* 2 cloves garlic, minced
* 2 tbsp olive oil
* 1 tsp ground cumin
* 1 tsp smoked paprika
* salt and pepper to taste
* fresh parsley, chopped, for garnish

Preparation:

1. Begin by slicing the aubergines lengthwise and scoop out a portion of the flesh to create a cavity, leaving about a 1cm border.
2. Dice the scooped aubergine flesh and set aside.
3. Drizzle the aubergine shells with a tablespoon of olive oil and season with salt and pepper.
4. Preheat the air fryer to 180°C.
5. Place the aubergine shells in the air fryer basket and cook for 10 minutes.
6. Meanwhile, heat the remaining olive oil in a pan over medium heat. Add the chopped red onion, garlic, and red pepper. Sauté until softened.
7. Stir in the diced aubergine flesh, ground cumin, and smoked paprika. Cook for another 5 minutes.
8. Pour in the couscous and vegetable stock, then cover the pan and remove from heat. Allow it to sit for 5 minutes, letting the couscous absorb the liquid.
9. Fluff the couscous with a fork and mix in the crumbled feta cheese. Adjust seasoning with salt and pepper.
10. Evenly distribute the couscous mixture into the pre-cooked aubergine shells.
11. Return the stuffed aubergines to the air fryer and cook for a further 15 minutes, until the tops are golden and crispy.
12. Serve hot, garnished with chopped fresh parsley.

NUTRITION FACTS PER 100G:
Energy: 117 kcal | Protein: 3g | Total Fat: 7g | Saturated Fat: 2g
Carbohydrates: 11g | Sugars: 2g | Dietary Fibre: 3g

Grilled Cauliflower Steaks with Pesto

SERVINGS: 2 | DIFFICULTY: EASY | TEMPERATURE: 200°C
PREPARATION TIME: 10 MINUTES | COOKING TIME: 20 MINUTES

Ingredients:

* 1 large cauliflower (about 600g), cut into 2cm thick steaks
* 60ml olive oil
* salt, to taste
* black pepper, to taste
* 100g fresh basil leaves
* 30g pine nuts, toasted
* 2 tbsp nutritional yeast
* 2 garlic cloves, peeled
* 80ml extra virgin olive oil
* juice of 1 lemon

Preparation:

1. Begin by preheating your air fryer to 200°C.
2. Drizzle olive oil evenly over the cauliflower steaks, ensuring they are well coated. Sprinkle with salt and black pepper to season.
3. Arrange the cauliflower steaks in the air fryer basket in a single layer, working in batches if necessary.
4. Cook the cauliflower in the air fryer for 15-20 minutes, flipping halfway through, until golden brown and tender.
5. Meanwhile, prepare the pesto. Combine the basil leaves, toasted pine nuts, nutritional yeast, and garlic cloves in a food processor.
6. Gradually add the extra virgin olive oil while processing the mixture until you achieve a smooth consistency. Add lemon juice, and season with salt and pepper to taste.
7. Once the cauliflower steaks are cooked, remove them from the air fryer and transfer to serving plates.
8. Generously spoon the pesto over the grilled cauliflower steaks before serving.

NUTRITION FACTS PER 100G:
Energy: 235 kcal | Protein: 4g | Total Fat: 23g | Saturated Fat: 3g
Carbohydrates: 3g | Sugars: 1g | Dietary Fibre: 3g

Air Fryer Falafel with Hummus Dip

SERVINGS: 4 | DIFFICULTY: MEDIUM | TEMPERATURE: 180°C
PREPARATION TIME: 20 MINUTES | COOKING TIME: 15 MINUTES

Ingredients:

* 400g canned chickpeas, drained and rinsed
* 1 small onion, chopped
* 3 cloves garlic, minced
* 60g fresh parsley, chopped
* 60g fresh coriander, chopped
* 2 tsp ground cumin
* 1 tsp ground coriander
* 1 tsp baking powder
* 3 tbsp plain flour
* salt and freshly ground black pepper, to taste
* 2 tbsp olive oil

For the hummus dip:

* 250g canned chickpeas, drained and rinsed
* 3 tbsp tahini
* 2 tbsp lemon juice
* 2 cloves garlic, minced
* 60ml olive oil
* salt, to taste
* water, as needed for consistency

Preparation:

1. Start by placing the chickpeas, onion, garlic, parsley, and coriander in a food processor. Pulse until roughly combined.
2. Add the ground cumin, ground coriander, baking powder, plain flour, salt, and pepper to the mixture. Process again until a coarse paste forms.
3. Form the mixture into small balls, about the size of a walnut, and slightly flatten them to form patties.
4. Preheat your air fryer to 180°C.
5. Lightly brush the falafel patties with olive oil on both sides.
6. Place the patties in the air fryer basket in a single layer; cook for 12-15 minutes, flipping halfway through, until golden and crispy.
7. While the falafel cooks, prepare the hummus dip. In a food processor, combine chickpeas, tahini, lemon juice, garlic, and salt.
8. Blend the mixture while gradually adding olive oil and water until smooth and creamy.
9. Serve the falafel warm with a side of hummus dip.

NUTRITION FACTS PER 100G:
Energy: 200 kcal | Protein: 6g | Total Fat: 12g | Saturated Fat: 2g
Carbohydrates: 18g | Sugars: 1g | Dietary Fibre: 6g

Roasted Butternut Squash with Quinoa and Herbs

SERVINGS: 4 | DIFFICULTY: EASY | TEMPERATURE: 180°C
PREPARATION TIME: 15 MINUTES | COOKING TIME: 25 MINUTES

Ingredients:

* 500g butternut squash, peeled and cubed
* 200g quinoa
* 2 tbsp olive oil
* 1 tsp ground cumin
* salt and black pepper to taste
* 1 red onion, finely chopped
* 1 red pepper, diced
* 2 cloves garlic, minced
* 50g fresh parsley, chopped
* 50g fresh coriander, chopped
* juice of 1 lemon
* 30g pumpkin seeds

Preparation:

1. First, rinse the quinoa under cold water. In a saucepan, bring 400ml of water to a boil. Add the quinoa and a pinch of salt, then reduce the heat to a simmer. Cover and cook for 15 minutes, or until the quinoa is fluffy and water is absorbed. Set aside.
2. While the quinoa cooks, place the butternut squash in a mixing bowl. Drizzle with olive oil and sprinkle with cumin, salt, and pepper. Toss to evenly coat the cubes.
3. Transfer the seasoned squash to the air fryer basket. Cook at 180°C for 20 minutes, shaking the basket halfway through, until the squash is tender and lightly caramelised.
4. In a large mixing bowl, combine the cooked quinoa, roasted butternut squash, chopped red onion, red pepper, and minced garlic.
5. Add the chopped parsley and coriander to the quinoa mixture. Squeeze in the lemon juice, adjusting seasoning with additional salt and pepper if desired.
6. Finally, sprinkle the pumpkin seeds over the top for added crunch and serve immediately.

> **NUTRITION FACTS PER 100G:**
> Energy: 144 kcal | Protein: 4g | Total Fat: 5g | Saturated Fat: 1g
> Carbohydrates: 19g | Sugars: 2g | Dietary Fibre: 3g

Air Fryer Halloumi Fries with Sweet Chilli Sauce

SERVINGS: 4 | DIFFICULTY: EASY | TEMPERATURE: 180°C
PREPARATION TIME: 10 MINUTES | COOKING TIME: 12 MINUTES

Ingredients:

* 250g halloumi cheese
* 4 tbsp plain flour
* 1 tsp smoked paprika
* 1 tsp garlic powder
* 1 tsp mixed herbs
* 2 tbsp olive oil
* 200ml sweet chilli sauce
* fresh coriander leaves for garnish (optional)

Preparation:

1. Begin by slicing the halloumi cheese into fries, approximately 1cm thick.
2. In a shallow bowl, mix together the plain flour, smoked paprika, garlic powder, and mixed herbs.
3. Coat the halloumi fries in the seasoned flour mixture, ensuring an even coating all around.
4. Lightly brush the coated halloumi fries with olive oil on all sides.
5. Preheat the air fryer to 180°C for 3 minutes.
6. Place the halloumi fries in the air fryer basket in a single layer, ensuring they do not touch.
7. Cook the fries in the air fryer for 12 minutes, flipping them halfway through, until they are golden brown and crispy.
8. Once cooked, carefully remove the halloumi fries from the air fryer.
9. Arrange the fries on a serving plate and serve with sweet chilli sauce on the side.
10. Garnish with fresh coriander leaves if desired.

NUTRITION FACTS PER 100G:
Energy: 258 kcal | Protein: 11g | Total Fat: 18g | Saturated Fat: 9g
Carbohydrates: 15g | Sugars: 6g | Dietary Fibre: 1g

Crispy Tofu Bites with Soy Dip

SERVINGS: 4 | DIFFICULTY: EASY | TEMPERATURE: 180°C
PREPARATION TIME: 15 MINUTES | COOKING TIME: 20 MINUTES

Ingredients:

* 400g firm tofu, drained and pressed
* 2 tbsp soy sauce
* 2 tbsp cornflour
* 1 tbsp olive oil
* 1 tsp garlic powder
* 1 tsp smoked paprika
* 1/2 tsp black pepper
* 2 tbsp sesame seeds
* 50ml soy sauce (for dipping)
* 1 tbsp rice vinegar
* 1 tbsp maple syrup
* 1 tsp grated fresh ginger
* 1 tbsp finely chopped spring onions
* fresh coriander for garnish

Preparation:

1. Begin by cutting the drained tofu into bite-sized cubes.
2. In a medium bowl, mix together 2 tablespoons of soy sauce, cornflour, olive oil, garlic powder, smoked paprika, and black pepper to create a marinade.
3. Add the tofu cubes to the marinade and gently toss until each piece is well-coated. Set aside to marinate for 10 minutes.
4. Preheat your air fryer to 180°C.
5. Once preheated, arrange the marinated tofu cubes in a single layer in the air fryer basket. Cook for 15-20 minutes, shaking the basket halfway through to ensure even cooking.
6. Just a few minutes before the tofu is done cooking, sprinkle 2 tablespoons of sesame seeds over the tofu cubes and continue crisping them up.
7. While the tofu is cooking, prepare the dipping sauce by whisking together 50ml of soy sauce, rice vinegar, maple syrup, and grated fresh ginger in a small bowl.
8. Pour the dipping sauce into individual ramekins and top with finely chopped spring onions.
9. Once the tofu bites are golden and crispy, remove them from the air fryer and serve immediately, garnished with fresh coriander.

NUTRITION FACTS PER 100G:
Energy: 150 kcal | Protein: 9g | Total Fat: 8g | Saturated Fat: 1g
Carbohydrates: 10g | Sugars: 2g | Dietary Fibre: 2g

Grilled Vegetable Skewers with Halloumi

SERVINGS: 4 | DIFFICULTY: EASY | TEMPERATURE: 180°C
PREPARATION TIME: 20 MINUTES | COOKING TIME: 15 MINUTES

Ingredients:

* 200g halloumi cheese, cut into thick cubes
* 1 red bell pepper, cut into chunks
* 1 yellow bell pepper, cut into chunks
* 1 courgette, sliced into thick rounds
* 150g cherry tomatoes
* 1 red onion, cut into wedges
* 3 tbsp olive oil
* 1 tbsp lemon juice
* 1 tsp dried oregano
* salt and pepper, to taste
* fresh basil leaves, to garnish

Preparation:

1. Begin by soaking wooden skewers in water for about 15 minutes to prevent burning.
2. In a large mixing bowl, combine olive oil, lemon juice, dried oregano, salt, and pepper to create a marinade.
3. Add the halloumi cubes, red and yellow bell peppers, courgette slices, cherry tomatoes, and red onion wedges to the bowl.
4. Toss the vegetables and halloumi thoroughly in the marinade, ensuring all pieces are evenly coated.
5. Thread a mixture of vegetables and halloumi onto each skewer, alternating between the different items for variety.
6. Preheat your air fryer to 180°C.
7. Once ready, arrange the skewers in the air fryer basket, making sure not to overcrowd.
8. Cook in the air fryer for 12-15 minutes, turning halfway through, until the vegetables are tender and slightly charred, and the halloumi is golden.
9. Remove the skewers carefully from the air fryer and place them onto a serving platter.
10. Garnish with fresh basil leaves before serving for an added burst of flavour.

NUTRITION FACTS PER 100G:
Energy: 140 kcal | Protein: 7g | Total Fat: 11g | Saturated Fat: 6g
Carbohydrates: 5g | Sugars: 3g | Dietary Fibre: 2g

Lentil Shepherd's Pie with Crispy Topping

SERVINGS: 4 | DIFFICULTY: MEDIUM | TEMPERATURE: 180°C
PREPARATION TIME: 20 MINUTES | COOKING TIME: 30 MINUTES

Ingredients:

* 250g green lentils, rinsed and drained
* 1 tbsp olive oil
* 1 onion, finely chopped
* 2 carrots, diced
* 2 celery sticks, chopped
* 2 garlic cloves, minced
* 400g tin chopped tomatoes
* 2 tbsp tomato purée
* 1 tsp dried thyme
* 1 tsp dried rosemary
* 500ml vegetable stock
* salt and pepper, to taste
* 500g potatoes, peeled and cut into chunks
* 2 tbsp unsweetened almond milk
* 2 tbsp nutritional yeast
* 1 tbsp vegan butter
* fresh parsley, chopped, for garnish

Preparation:

1. To begin, place the lentils in a saucepan, cover with water, and bring to a boil. Simmer for 15 minutes or until tender but not mushy. Drain and set aside.
2. Meanwhile, heat olive oil in a pan over medium heat. Sauté the onion, carrots, and celery for about 5 minutes or until softened.
3. Incorporate the garlic and cook for another minute, stirring frequently.
4. Add in the chopped tomatoes, tomato purée, thyme, rosemary, and vegetable stock. Bring the mixture to a boil, then reduce the heat and let it simmer for 10 minutes.
5. Stir the cooked lentils into the vegetable mixture. Season with salt and pepper according to your taste.
6. In the meantime, boil the potatoes in a separate saucepan for 15 minutes until soft. Drain and mash with almond milk, nutritional yeast, and vegan butter.
7. Preheat your air fryer to 180°C. Transfer the lentil mixture into a baking dish that fits inside your air fryer.
8. Spoon the mashed potatoes over the lentil mixture, spreading evenly.
9. Cook in the air fryer for 15 minutes or until the topping is golden and crispy.
10. Sprinkle with chopped parsley before serving to add a burst of freshness.

NUTRITION FACTS PER 100G:
Energy: 80 kcal | Protein: 4g | Total Fat: 2g | Saturated Fat: 0g
Carbohydrates: 12g | Sugars: 3g | Dietary Fibre: 3g

Mushroom and Spinach Wellington

SERVINGS: 4 | DIFFICULTY: MEDIUM | TEMPERATURE: 180°C
PREPARATION TIME: 20 MINUTES | COOKING TIME: 25 MINUTES

Ingredients:

* 1 sheet of puff pastry (vegan)
* 250g chestnut mushrooms, finely chopped
* 2 cloves of garlic, minced
* 1 onion, finely diced
* 100g fresh spinach
* 1 tbsp olive oil
* 1 tbsp soy sauce
* 1 tsp thyme
* 1 tsp rosemary
* salt and pepper, to taste
* 2 tbsp almond milk (for brushing)

Preparation:

1. Begin by heating the olive oil in a pan over medium heat. Sauté the onion and garlic until they become soft and translucent.
2. Next, add the chopped mushrooms to the pan. Cook until the mushrooms are golden and have released their moisture, about 5 minutes.
3. Stir in the soy sauce, thyme, and rosemary. Allow the mixture to cook for another 2 minutes, then add the fresh spinach. Cook until the spinach wilts, and season with salt and pepper.
4. Roll out the puff pastry on a floured surface. Place the mushroom and spinach mixture in the centre, spreading it out evenly.
5. Carefully fold the pastry over the filling, sealing the edges. Transfer to the air fryer basket with the seam side down.
6. Lightly brush the top with almond milk, which will help it achieve a golden colour.
7. Cook in the air fryer at 180°C for 25 minutes or until the pastry is crisp and golden.
8. Allow to cool slightly before slicing into generous portions. Serve warm for best enjoyment.

NUTRITION FACTS PER 100G:
Energy: 150 kcal | Protein: 3g | Total Fat: 9g | Saturated Fat: 2g
Carbohydrates: 15g | Sugars: 1g | Dietary Fibre: 2g

Courgette Fritters with Mint Yoghurt

SERVINGS: 4 | DIFFICULTY: EASY | TEMPERATURE: 180°C
PREPARATION TIME: 15 MINUTES | COOKING TIME: 12 MINUTES

Ingredients:

* 500g courgettes, grated
* 1 tsp salt
* 100g plain flour
* 1 tsp baking powder
* 1/2 tsp ground cumin
* 1/2 tsp smoked paprika
* 2 spring onions, finely chopped
* 1 tbsp fresh coriander, chopped
* 1 tbsp fresh mint, chopped
* 2 tbsp olive oil
* 150ml plain yoghurt
* salt and pepper to taste

Preparation:

1. Mix the grated courgettes with 1 tsp of salt and let them sit for 10 minutes to draw out excess moisture.
2. After 10 minutes, squeeze the courgettes in a clean tea towel to remove as much moisture as possible.
3. In a large mixing bowl, combine the courgettes, flour, baking powder, cumin, smoked paprika, spring onions, and chopped coriander.
4. Shape the mixture into small, flat fritters using your hands.
5. Preheat the air fryer to 180°C.
6. Brush the air fryer basket with 1 tbsp of olive oil to prevent sticking.
7. Arrange the fritters in the basket, leaving a little space between each one.
8. Air fry the fritters for about 12 minutes, flipping them halfway through, until they are golden and crisp.
9. In a small bowl, mix the yoghurt with chopped mint, and season with salt and pepper to taste.
10. Serve the fritters hot, accompanied by the mint yoghurt.

NUTRITION FACTS PER 100G:
Energy: 120 kcal | Protein: 3g | Total Fat: 7g | Saturated Fat: 1g
Carbohydrates: 13g | Sugars: 2g | Dietary Fibre: 2g

Aubergine Parmigiana with a Crunchy Top

SERVINGS: 4 | DIFFICULTY: MEDIUM | TEMPERATURE: 180°C
PREPARATION TIME: 20 MINUTES | COOKING TIME: 25 MINUTES

Ingredients:

* 2 medium aubergines, sliced into 1cm rounds
* 2 tbsp olive oil
* 1 onion, finely chopped
* 2 garlic cloves, minced
* 400g tin chopped tomatoes
* 1 tsp dried oregano
* salt and pepper, to taste
* 80g vegan mozzarella, shredded
* 50g breadcrumbs
* 2 tbsp nutritional yeast
* fresh basil leaves, for garnish

Preparation:

1. Preheat the air fryer to 180°C. Lightly brush aubergine slices with olive oil on both sides. Air fry the slices in batches for 10 minutes, flipping halfway through, until golden brown.
2. In a frying pan, heat 1tbsp of olive oil over medium heat. Sauté the onion and garlic until soft and fragrant, about 5 minutes.
3. Stir in the chopped tomatoes and oregano, then season with salt and pepper. Simmer the sauce on low heat for 10 minutes, allowing the flavours to meld together.
4. In a baking dish that fits your air fryer, layer half of the aubergine slices. Cover with half of the tomato sauce and sprinkle half of the vegan mozzarella on top.
5. Repeat with the remaining aubergine slices, tomato sauce, and mozzarella.
6. Mix together breadcrumbs and nutritional yeast in a small bowl, then sprinkle the mixture evenly over the top layer.
7. Carefully place the baking dish in the air fryer and cook for 15 minutes, or until the top is golden and crispy.
8. Garnish with fresh basil leaves before serving. Serve hot and enjoy this comforting dish.

NUTRITION FACTS PER 100G:
Energy: 129 kcal | Protein: 3g | Total Fat: 8g | Saturated Fat: 1g
Carbohydrates: 12g | Sugars: 4g | Dietary Fibre: 4g

Chickpea and Spinach Patties with Tahini

SERVINGS: 4 | DIFFICULTY: EASY | TEMPERATURE: 180°C
PREPARATION TIME: 15 MINUTES | COOKING TIME: 15 MINUTES

Ingredients:

* 400g canned chickpeas, drained and rinsed
* 100g fresh spinach leaves
* 1 small onion, finely chopped
* 3 tbsp fresh coriander, chopped
* 1 tbsp lemon juice
* 2 tbsp plain flour
* 2 cloves garlic, minced
* 1 tsp ground cumin
* 1 tsp smoked paprika
* salt and pepper to taste
* olive oil spray

For the Tahini Sauce:

* 4 tbsp tahini
* 2 tbsp lemon juice
* 2 tbsp water
* 1 clove garlic, minced
* salt to taste

Preparation:

1. Begin by placing the chickpeas, spinach, onion, coriander, lemon juice, flour, garlic, cumin, smoked paprika, salt, and pepper into a food processor. Blend the mixture until it reaches a chunky paste consistency.
2. Shape the chickpea mixture into eight equal-sized patties using your hands.
3. Preheat your air fryer to 180°C. Lightly spray the air fryer basket with olive oil.
4. Arrange the patties in the air fryer basket in a single layer, ensuring they do not touch. Spray the tops of the patties with a little more olive oil.
5. Cook the patties for 7-8 minutes, then flip them over and continue cooking for another 7-8 minutes, until golden brown and crisp.
6. While the patties are cooking, prepare the tahini sauce. Mix the tahini, lemon juice, water, garlic, and salt in a small bowl until smooth.
7. Once the patties are done, serve them warm with a drizzle of the tahini sauce on top.

NUTRITION FACTS PER 100G:
Energy: 170 kcal | Protein: 6g | Total Fat: 9g | Saturated Fat: 2g
Carbohydrates: 16g | Sugars: 2g | Dietary Fibre: 5g

Crispy Roasted Sweet Potato Wedges

SERVINGS: 4 | DIFFICULTY: EASY | TEMPERATURE: 200°C
PREPARATION TIME: 10 MINUTES | COOKING TIME: 20 MINUTES

Ingredients:

* 600g sweet potatoes
* 2 tbsp olive oil
* 1 tsp smoked paprika
* 1 tsp garlic powder
* 1/2 tsp salt
* 1/4 tsp black pepper
* 1 tbsp fresh parsley, chopped (optional)

Preparation:

1. Begin by washing and scrubbing the sweet potatoes thoroughly. Cut them into wedges, around 1-1.5cm thick, ensuring even sizes for consistent cooking.
2. Place the sweet potato wedges in a large bowl. Drizzle with olive oil, then sprinkle with smoked paprika, garlic powder, salt, and black pepper.
3. Toss the wedges well, ensuring each piece is evenly coated with the oil and seasoning mixture.
4. Preheat the air fryer to 200°C for a couple of minutes. Once preheated, arrange the sweet potato wedges in a single layer in the air fryer basket. It's important not to overcrowd the basket; work in batches if necessary.
5. Cook the wedges for about 10 minutes, then remove the basket and shake it gently. Return it to the air fryer and continue cooking for an additional 10 minutes, or until the wedges are crispy and golden brown.
6. Remove the sweet potato wedges from the air fryer. If desired, garnish with fresh parsley before serving immediately.

NUTRITION FACTS PER 100G:
Energy: 140 kcal | Protein: 2g | Total Fat: 6g | Saturated Fat: 1g
Carbohydrates: 21g | Sugars: 5g | Dietary Fibre: 3g

Air Fryer Stuffed Peppers with Rice and Vegetables

SERVINGS: 4 | DIFFICULTY: MEDIUM | TEMPERATURE: 180°C
PREPARATION TIME: 20 MINUTES | COOKING TIME: 25 MINUTES

Ingredients:

* 4 large bell peppers
* 200g cooked rice
* 150g cooked mixed vegetables (peas, carrots, and sweetcorn)
* 1 onion, finely chopped
* 2 cloves garlic, minced
* 2 tbsp olive oil
* 1 tsp smoked paprika
* 1 tsp cumin
* 1 tbsp tomato purée
* salt, to taste
* pepper, to taste
* fresh coriander, chopped, for garnish

Preparation:

1. Start by preheating the air fryer to 180°C.
2. Cut the tops off the bell peppers and carefully remove the seeds and membranes.
3. Heat olive oil in a pan over medium heat, then sauté the onion and garlic until translucent.
4. Stir in the cooked rice, mixed vegetables, smoked paprika, cumin, and tomato purée, ensuring everything is well combined.
5. Season the mixture with salt and pepper to your liking.
6. Stuff the prepared peppers with the rice and vegetable mixture, pressing down gently to pack them tightly.
7. Place the stuffed peppers in the air fryer basket, ensuring they do not tip over during cooking.
8. Cook in the air fryer for 25 minutes or until the peppers are tender and slightly charred on the edges.
9. Once cooked, carefully remove the peppers from the air fryer.
10. Garnish with fresh chopped coriander before serving.

> **NUTRITION FACTS PER 100G:**
> Energy: 105 kcal | Protein: 3g | Total Fat: 5g | Saturated Fat: 1g
> Carbohydrates: 14g | Sugars: 4g | Dietary Fibre: 3g

Grilled Portobello Mushrooms with Garlic and Cheese

SERVINGS: 4 | DIFFICULTY: EASY | TEMPERATURE: 200°C
PREPARATION TIME: 10 MINUTES | COOKING TIME: 15 MINUTES

Ingredients:

* 4 large portobello mushrooms
* 2 tbsp olive oil
* 2 cloves garlic, minced
* 50g vegan cheese, shredded
* 1 tbsp balsamic vinegar
* 1 tbsp fresh parsley, chopped
* salt, to taste
* black pepper, to taste

Preparation:

1. Begin by cleaning the portobello mushrooms with a damp cloth and removing the stems.
2. In a small bowl, combine olive oil, minced garlic, balsamic vinegar, salt, and pepper.
3. Brush the mushroom caps generously with the garlic oil mixture, ensuring the gills are coated well.
4. Preheat the air fryer to 200°C to allow for even cooking.
5. Arrange the mushrooms in the air fryer basket, gill side up, ensuring they do not overlap.
6. Air fry the mushrooms for 10 minutes, keeping an eye on them to prevent overcooking.
7. Carefully remove the basket, sprinkle the mushrooms with the shredded vegan cheese, and return to the air fryer.
8. Continue to air fry for an additional 5 minutes or until the cheese has melted beautifully.
9. Finish by garnishing with chopped parsley before serving.
10. Serve warm and enjoy the delightful flavours.

NUTRITION FACTS PER 100G:
Energy: 121 kcal | Protein: 3g | Total Fat: 9g | Saturated Fat: 2g
Carbohydrates: 6g | Sugars: 2g | Dietary Fibre: 2g

Chapter 6:
Sweet Treats and Desserts

Air Fryer Victoria Sponge Bites

SERVINGS: 12 | DIFFICULTY: EASY | TEMPERATURE: 180°C
PREPARATION TIME: 15 MINUTES | COOKING TIME: 10 MINUTES

Ingredients:

* 100g self-raising flour
* 100g caster sugar
* 100g unsalted butter, softened
* 2 large eggs
* 1 tsp vanilla extract
* 2 tbsp milk
* 100g raspberry jam
* 150ml double cream
* 1 tbsp icing sugar

Preparation:

1. Begin by preheating the air fryer to 180°C.
2. Cream together the caster sugar and unsalted butter until light and fluffy.
3. Add the eggs one at a time, mixing well after each addition.
4. Stir in the vanilla extract and milk until fully incorporated.
5. Gently fold in the self-raising flour until a smooth batter forms.
6. Divide the batter evenly into silicone moulds, filling each halfway.
7. Carefully place the moulds in the air fryer basket.
8. Bake for 10 minutes or until the sponge bites spring back when touched.
9. Once cooled, slice each bite horizontally and spread a layer of raspberry jam in the centre.
10. Whip the double cream until soft peaks form and dollop over the jam layer.
11. Finish by dusting the tops with icing sugar before serving.

NUTRITION FACTS PER 100G:
Energy: 365 kcal | Protein: 5g | Total Fat: 23g | Saturated Fat: 14g
Carbohydrates: 38g | Sugars: 24g | Dietary Fibre: 1g

Sticky Toffee Pudding with Caramel Sauce

SERVINGS: 6 | DIFFICULTY: MEDIUM | TEMPERATURE: 180°C
PREPARATION TIME: 15 MINUTES | COOKING TIME: 25 MINUTES

Ingredients:

* 175g dates, pitted and chopped
* 150ml boiling water
* 1 tsp bicarbonate of soda
* 85g unsalted butter, softened
* 85g light muscovado sugar
* 2 tbsp golden syrup
* 2 tbsp black treacle

* 2 large eggs
* 200g self-raising flour

For the caramel sauce:
* 100g light muscovado sugar
* 100g unsalted butter
* 2 tbsp double cream

Preparation:

1. Begin by soaking the dates in boiling water and stir in the bicarbonate of soda. Allow to sit for 10 minutes.
2. Meanwhile, in a mixing bowl, cream together the softened butter and light muscovado sugar until light and fluffy.
3. Incorporate the golden syrup, black treacle, and eggs into the sugar mixture, beating well after each addition.
4. Gradually fold in the self-raising flour until fully combined.
5. Add the soaked dates along with any liquid to the mixture, stirring until even.
6. Lightly grease and line a suitable tin fitting your air fryer basket.
7. Pour the batter into the prepared tin, smoothing the top with a spatula.
8. Preheat the air fryer to 180°C and place the tin in the basket.
9. Cook the pudding for 25 minutes, or until a skewer inserted into the centre comes out clean.
10. For the caramel sauce, place the sugar, butter, and double cream in a saucepan over medium heat.
11. Stir continuously until the butter has melted and the sugar dissolved, creating a smooth sauce.
12. Once the pudding is ready, remove it from the air fryer and allow it to cool slightly.
13. Drizzle generously with caramel sauce before serving.

> **NUTRITION FACTS PER 100G:**
> Energy: 380 kcal | Protein: 3g | Total Fat: 17g | Saturated Fat: 10g
> Carbohydrates: 55g | Sugars: 45g | Dietary Fibre: 2g

Apple and Cinnamon Turnovers

SERVINGS: 4 | DIFFICULTY: EASY | TEMPERATURE: 180°C
PREPARATION TIME: 15 MINUTES | COOKING TIME: 12 MINUTES

Ingredients:

* 250g puff pastry
* 2 medium apples, peeled, cored, and diced
* 2 tbsp light brown sugar
* 1 tsp ground cinnamon
* 1 tbsp lemon juice
* 1 tbsp plain flour
* 1 egg, beaten
* icing sugar for dusting

Preparation:

1. Begin by mixing the diced apples, light brown sugar, cinnamon, lemon juice, and plain flour in a bowl until well combined.
2. Unroll the puff pastry on a floured surface and cut into 8 equal squares.
3. Place a spoonful of the apple mixture in the centre of each puff pastry square.
4. Brush the edges of the pastry squares with the beaten egg.
5. Fold each square diagonally to form a triangle, pressing the edges to seal tightly.
6. Arrange the turnovers in the air fryer basket, leaving a small gap between each.
7. Lightly brush the tops with more beaten egg.
8. Set the air fryer to 180°C and cook the turnovers for 12 minutes or until golden and puffed.
9. Once done, carefully remove the turnovers and allow them to cool slightly on a wire rack.
10. Just before serving, dust with icing sugar and enjoy warm.

NUTRITION FACTS PER 100G:
Energy: 265 kcal | Protein: 3g | Total Fat: 16g | Saturated Fat: 8g
Carbohydrates: 27g | Sugars: 11g | Dietary Fibre: 1g

Jam Doughnuts with Raspberry Filling

SERVINGS: 8 | DIFFICULTY: MEDIUM | TEMPERATURE: 180°C
PREPARATION TIME: 20 MINUTES | COOKING TIME: 10 MINUTES

Ingredients:

* 250g strong white bread flour
* 50g caster sugar
* 7g instant yeast
* 1/2 tsp salt
* 100ml whole milk, warmed
* 1 large egg
* 40g unsalted butter, softened
* 100g raspberry jam
* 1 tsp vanilla extract
* 50g granulated sugar for coating
* cooking spray

Preparation:

1. Begin by mixing the flour, caster sugar, yeast, and salt in a large bowl. Create a well in the centre.
2. Combine the warmed milk, egg, and vanilla extract, then pour it into the well of dry ingredients. Mix to form a dough.
3. Introduce the softened butter gradually, kneading until the dough is smooth and elastic. This should take around 5-7 minutes.
4. Cover the dough with a damp cloth and let it rise in a warm place until it doubles in size, approximately 1 hour.
5. Once risen, punch down the dough and divide it into 8 equal pieces. Shape each piece into a ball and flatten slightly.
6. Preheat the air fryer to 180°C.
7. Spray the air fryer basket with cooking spray and place the doughnuts inside, allowing space for expansion. You may need to cook in batches.
8. Cook the doughnuts in the air fryer for about 5 minutes on each side, or until golden brown and cooked through.
9. Whilst the doughnuts are still warm, roll them in granulated sugar until evenly coated.
10. Using a skewer, create a small hole in each doughnut and pipe the raspberry jam into the centre.
11. Serve warm and enjoy.

NUTRITION FACTS PER 100G:
Energy: 309 kcal | Protein: 7g | Total Fat: 8g | Saturated Fat: 5g
Carbohydrates: 51g | Sugars: 19g | Dietary Fibre: 1g

Bakewell Tartlets with Almond Icing

SERVINGS: 8 | DIFFICULTY: MEDIUM | TEMPERATURE: 180°C
PREPARATION TIME: 20 MINUTES | COOKING TIME: 15 MINUTES

Ingredients:

* 150g plain flour
* 50g caster sugar
* 100g unsalted butter, cold and cubed
* 1 large egg yolk
* 1-2 tbsp cold water
* 100g ground almonds
* 100g icing sugar
* 100g raspberry jam
* 1 tsp almond extract
* 50g flaked almonds
* 2-3 tbsp water (for icing)

Preparation:

1. Begin by preparing the pastry. Combine plain flour and caster sugar in a bowl. Mix in the butter using your fingertips until the mixture resembles breadcrumbs.
2. Incorporate the egg yolk and 1 tbsp of cold water, mixing to form a dough. Add an extra tbsp of water if necessary. Wrap in cling film and refrigerate for 15 minutes.
3. Roll out the chilled dough on a floured surface. Cut out circles using a cutter to fit moulds in your air fryer basket. Gently press into place.
4. Spoon a layer of raspberry jam into each pastry case, followed by a sprinkle of ground almonds.
5. Preheat the air fryer to 180°C.
6. Bake the tarts in the preheated air fryer for 10 minutes. Scatter flaked almonds on top.
7. For the icing, blend icing sugar with almond extract and water until smooth.
8. Allow the tarts to cool slightly before drizzling with almond icing.
9. Prior to serving, let the icing set for a short while.

NUTRITION FACTS PER 100G:
Energy: 450 kcal | Protein: 6g | Total Fat: 26g | Saturated Fat: 9g
Carbohydrates: 46g | Sugars: 30g | Dietary Fibre: 2g

Air Fryer Lemon Drizzle Cake Slices

SERVINGS: 8 SLICES | DIFFICULTY: EASY | TEMPERATURE: 180°C
PREPARATION TIME: 15 MINUTES | COOKING TIME: 25 MINUTES

Ingredients:

* 150g unsalted butter, softened
* 150g caster sugar
* 2 large eggs
* 150g self-raising flour
* zest of 1 lemon
* 3 tbsp milk
* 100g icing sugar
* juice of 1 lemon

Preparation:

1. Begin by preheating your air fryer to 180°C.
2. In a mixing bowl, cream together the softened butter and caster sugar until light and fluffy.
3. Crack the eggs into the mixture, one at a time, beating well after each addition.
4. Gently fold in the self-raising flour and lemon zest, ensuring the batter is smooth.
5. Stir in the milk until the mixture reaches a smooth consistency.
6. Grease a small square baking pan that fits in your air fryer, then pour the batter into the prepared pan.
7. Place the pan into the air fryer basket and cook for 25 minutes or until a skewer inserted into the centre comes out clean.
8. Meanwhile, in a small bowl, mix the icing sugar with lemon juice to create the drizzle.
9. Once the cake is cooked, remove it from the air fryer and let it cool for a few minutes.
10. Drizzle the lemon icing over the cooled cake, allowing it to set before slicing.
11. Finally, cut the cake into slices and serve.

NUTRITION FACTS PER 100G:
Energy: 380 kcal | Protein: 4g | Total Fat: 17g | Saturated Fat: 10g
Carbohydrates: 54g | Sugars: 36g | Dietary Fibre: 1g

Fudge Brownies with a Gooey Centre

SERVINGS: 9 | DIFFICULTY: MEDIUM | TEMPERATURE: 160°C
PREPARATION TIME: 15 MINUTES | COOKING TIME: 20 MINUTES

Ingredients:

* 150g dark chocolate
* 120g unsalted butter
* 200g caster sugar
* 2 large eggs
* 1 tsp vanilla extract

* 100g plain flour
* 25g cocoa powder
* 1/4 tsp salt
* 50g milk chocolate chunks
* 50g chopped nuts (optional)

Preparation:

1. Begin by melting the dark chocolate and unsalted butter together in a heatproof bowl over simmering water, stirring until smooth.
2. Once melted, remove the bowl from the heat, and allow the chocolate mixture to cool slightly.
3. In a separate large bowl, whisk together the caster sugar, eggs, and vanilla extract until light and frothy.
4. Gently fold the cooled chocolate mixture into the egg mixture, ensuring it's well combined.
5. In another bowl, sift together the plain flour, cocoa powder, and salt.
6. Gradually fold the dry ingredients into the chocolate and egg mixture, taking care not to overmix.
7. Incorporate the milk chocolate chunks and nuts (if using) into the batter.
8. Line the air fryer basket with parchment paper, making sure it covers the base and sides.
9. Pour the brownie mixture into the prepared basket, spreading it evenly.
10. Preheat the air fryer to 160°C and set the brownies to cook for 20 minutes.
11. Once cooked, let the brownies cool in the basket for 10 minutes before slicing.
12. Finally, enjoy these indulgent fudge brownies with their irresistible gooey centre.

NUTRITION FACTS PER 100G:
Energy: 450 kcal | Protein: 6g | Total Fat: 26g | Saturated Fat: 15g
Carbohydrates: 50g | Sugars: 37g | Dietary Fibre: 3g

Scones with Clotted Cream and Jam

SERVINGS: 8 | DIFFICULTY: MEDIUM | TEMPERATURE: 180°C
PREPARATION TIME: 15 MINUTES | COOKING TIME: 12 MINUTES

Ingredients:

* 350g self-raising flour
* 85g unsalted butter, chilled and cubed
* 3 tbsp caster sugar
* 175ml milk
* 1 tsp vanilla extract
* 1 egg, beaten
* pinch of salt
* clotted cream, for serving
* jam of your choice, for serving

Preparation:

1. Begin by preheating the air fryer to 180°C.
2. In a large mixing bowl, combine the self-raising flour and a pinch of salt. Add the chilled, cubed butter.
3. Rub the butter into the flour using your fingertips until the mixture resembles fine breadcrumbs.
4. Stir in the caster sugar. Make a well in the centre of the flour mixture.
5. Gently heat the milk in a pan until warm but not boiling. Remove from heat and add the vanilla extract.
6. Pour the warm milk mixture into the flour, then combine quickly with a cutlery knife to form a soft dough.
7. Turn the dough onto a lightly floured surface and knead briefly until smooth.
8. Roll out the dough to about 2.5cm thick. Use a 5cm cutter to cut out rounds of dough, re-rolling as necessary.
9. Arrange the scones in the air fryer basket, leaving some space between each.
10. Brush the tops with the beaten egg. Air fry for 12 minutes or until golden brown.
11. Allow the scones to cool slightly, then serve with clotted cream and your favourite jam.

NUTRITION FACTS PER 100G:
Energy: 270 kcal | Protein: 5g | Total Fat: 10g | Saturated Fat: 6g
Carbohydrates: 39g | Sugars: 6g | Dietary Fibre: 1g

Pear and Almond Tart

SERVINGS: 6 | DIFFICULTY: MEDIUM | TEMPERATURE: 180°C
PREPARATION TIME: 20 MINUTES | COOKING TIME: 25 MINUTES

Ingredients:

* 1 sheet of puff pastry (about 250g)
* 3 ripe pears, peeled, cored, and sliced
* 100g ground almonds
* 80g caster sugar
* 50g unsalted butter, softened
* 1 large egg
* 1 tsp vanilla extract
* 1 tbsp plain flour
* 1 tbsp lemon juice
* 2 tbsp flaked almonds
* 1 tbsp icing sugar for dusting

Preparation:

1. Begin by rolling out the puff pastry, ensuring it's even. Line the air fryer basket with a sheet of parchment paper and gently place the pastry inside, trimming any excess.
2. Combine the ground almonds, caster sugar, and flour in a mixing bowl. Stir in the softened butter, egg, and vanilla extract until a smooth paste forms.
3. Spread the almond mixture evenly over the pastry, leaving a small border around the edges.
4. Toss the pear slices in lemon juice, then arrange them over the almond filling in a fan-like pattern.
5. Sprinkle the flaked almonds on top of the pears for added texture.
6. Carefully place the prepared tart into the air fryer and set the temperature to 180°C. Cook for 25 minutes or until the pastry is golden and the pears are tender.
7. Once cooked, remove the tart from the air fryer and allow it to cool slightly. Finish by dusting with icing sugar before serving.

NUTRITION FACTS PER 100G:
Energy: 260 kcal | Protein: 4g | Total Fat: 16g | Saturated Fat: 5g
Carbohydrates: 26g | Sugars: 15g | Dietary Fibre: 2g

Eccles Cakes with Flaky Pastry

SERVINGS: 12 | DIFFICULTY: MODERATE | TEMPERATURE: 180°C
PREPARATION TIME: 30 MINUTES | COOKING TIME: 15 MINUTES

Ingredients:

* 225g plain flour
* 150g unsalted butter, cold and diced
* 50g icing sugar
* 1 egg yolk
* 2-3 tbsp cold water
* 100g currants
* 50g brown sugar
* 1 tsp mixed spice
* 30g unsalted butter, melted
* 1 tbsp milk
* granulated sugar for sprinkling

Preparation:

1. Begin by preparing the pastry. In a large bowl, combine the flour and diced butter. Rub the butter into the flour until the mixture resembles breadcrumbs.
2. Blend in the icing sugar. Add the egg yolk followed by 2 tbsp of cold water. Mix until the dough begins to come together, adding more water if necessary.
3. Shape the dough into a disc, wrap in cling film, and refrigerate for 20 minutes.
4. Next, make the filling. Mix together the currants, brown sugar, mixed spice, and melted butter. Set aside.
5. Once chilled, roll out the pastry on a floured surface to a thickness of about 3mm. Cut out 12 circles using a 10cm cutter.
6. Distribute a spoonful of the filling onto the centre of each pastry circle. Moisten the edges with a little water, then gather and pinch to encase the filling completely.
7. Turn the cakes over, gently press into a slightly flattened shape, and snip a small slit on top with scissors.
8. Brush each cake with milk and sprinkle with granulated sugar.
9. Preheat the air fryer to 180°C. Arrange the cakes in the air fryer basket in a single layer, working in batches if needed.
10. Cook for approximately 15 minutes until golden brown and crisp.
11. Allow the Eccles cakes to cool slightly on a wire rack before serving.

NUTRITION FACTS PER 100G:
Energy: 420 kcal | Protein: 3g | Total Fat: 22g | Saturated Fat: 14g
Carbohydrates: 54g | Sugars: 24g | Dietary Fibre: 2g

Rhubarb and Custard Crumble

SERVINGS: 4 | DIFFICULTY: MEDIUM | TEMPERATURE: 180°C
PREPARATION TIME: 15 MINUTES | COOKING TIME: 25 MINUTES

Ingredients:

* 300g rhubarb, chopped
* 100g caster sugar
* 1 tsp vanilla extract
* 300ml whole milk
* 50g custard powder

* 100g plain flour
* 75g rolled oats
* 75g unsalted butter, cubed
* 75g soft brown sugar
* 1 tsp ground cinnamon

Preparation:

1. Begin by preheating the air fryer to 180°C.
2. In a saucepan over medium heat, combine the chopped rhubarb and caster sugar. Stir continuously until the rhubarb softens and the sugar dissolves, approximately 5 minutes.
3. Introduce the vanilla extract to the rhubarb mixture and set aside.
4. In a separate saucepan, heat the whole milk until warm, then whisk in the custard powder until fully incorporated to form a smooth custard.
5. To create the crumble topping, mix the plain flour, rolled oats, and ground cinnamon in a large bowl. Rub in the cubed butter with your fingertips until the mixture resembles breadcrumbs.
6. Stir in the soft brown sugar to complete the crumble topping.
7. In individual ramekins, layer the rhubarb at the base, then pour over the custard.
8. Distribute the crumble topping evenly over each ramekin.
9. Position the ramekins in the air fryer basket, ensuring they are evenly spaced.
10. Cook in the air fryer for 20 to 25 minutes or until the crumble topping is golden and the filling is bubbling.
11. Serve warm and enjoy the delightful combination of tart rhubarb, creamy custard, and crunchy crumble.

NUTRITION FACTS PER 100G:
Energy: 220 kcal | Protein: 4g | Total Fat: 9g | Saturated Fat: 5g
Carbohydrates: 32g | Sugars: 20g | Dietary Fibre: 2g

Air Fryer Shortbread Fingers

SERVINGS: 12 | DIFFICULTY: EASY | TEMPERATURE: 170°C
PREPARATION TIME: 10 MINUTES | COOKING TIME: 12 MINUTES

Ingredients:

* 150g plain flour
* 100g unsalted butter, softened
* 50g caster sugar
* 1 tbsp cornflour
* a pinch of salt

Preparation:

1. Begin by preheating the air fryer to 170°C.
2. In a mixing bowl, combine the softened butter and caster sugar, creaming them together until light and fluffy.
3. Gradually sift in the plain flour, cornflour, and salt, mixing until the dough forms a crumbly texture.
4. Gather the dough, bringing it together with your hands until it forms a smooth ball.
5. Roll out the dough on a lightly floured surface to about 1cm thick.
6. Cut the dough into finger-sized strips, traditionally around 2cm wide and 8cm long.
7. Carefully place the shortbread fingers into the air fryer basket, ensuring they are spaced slightly apart.
8. Air fry the shortbread fingers for approximately 12 minutes or until they turn a light golden colour.
9. Once cooked, remove from the air fryer and allow them to cool on a wire rack.
10. Serve and enjoy your delicate, buttery shortbread fingers.

> **NUTRITION FACTS PER 100G:**
> Energy: 470 kcal | Protein: 4g | Total Fat: 28g | Saturated Fat: 18g
> Carbohydrates: 54g | Sugars: 15g | Dietary Fibre: 1g

Chocolate Chip Cookies with a Crispy Edge

SERVINGS: 12 COOKIES | DIFFICULTY: EASY | TEMPERATURE: 180°C
PREPARATION TIME: 15 MINUTES | COOKING TIME: 8 MINUTES

Ingredients:

* 150g plain flour
* 1/2 tsp bicarbonate of soda
* 1/4 tsp salt
* 100g unsalted butter, softened
* 75g caster sugar
* 75g light brown sugar
* 1 tsp vanilla extract
* 1 large egg
* 150g dark chocolate chips

Preparation:

1. Begin by preheating your air fryer to 180°C.
2. In a mixing bowl, combine the plain flour, bicarbonate of soda, and salt. Set aside.
3. In a large bowl, cream together the softened butter, caster sugar, and light brown sugar until the mixture is light and fluffy.
4. Incorporate the vanilla extract and the egg into the butter mixture, blending well until smooth.
5. Gradually add the dry ingredients to the wet mixture, stirring just until combined.
6. Fold in the dark chocolate chips, ensuring they are evenly distributed throughout the dough.
7. Using a tablespoon, scoop the dough and shape it into small balls.
8. Line the air fryer basket with baking paper, placing the dough balls slightly apart to allow for spreading.
9. Place the basket into the air fryer and bake the cookies for 8 minutes or until the edges are golden and crispy.
10. Allow the cookies to cool slightly in the air fryer before transferring them to a wire rack to cool completely.

NUTRITION FACTS PER 100G:
Energy: 475 kcal | Protein: 6g | Total Fat: 25g | Saturated Fat: 15g
Carbohydrates: 60g | Sugars: 35g | Dietary Fibre: 3g

Honeycomb Crunch Bars

SERVINGS: 8 | DIFFICULTY: MODERATE | TEMPERATURE: 160°C
PREPARATION TIME: 15 MINUTES | COOKING TIME: 20 MINUTES

Ingredients:

* 100g caster sugar
* 50g golden syrup
* 2 tsp bicarbonate of soda
* 200g milk chocolate, chopped
* 2 tbsp unsalted butter
* 50g crushed digestive biscuits

Preparation:

1. Begin by lining your air fryer basket with baking parchment.
2. Pour the caster sugar and golden syrup into a medium saucepan.
3. Gently heat the mixture over low heat until the sugar dissolves completely.
4. Increase the heat and bring the mixture to a boil without stirring for about 5 minutes until it turns a golden amber.
5. Quickly remove from heat and immediately whisk in the bicarbonate of soda until fully incorporated.
6. Spill the mixture into the prepared air fryer basket and allow it to cool and set.
7. Once set, break the honeycomb into bite-sized pieces.
8. While the honeycomb cools, melt the milk chocolate and butter together in a heatproof bowl over simmering water.
9. Stir occasionally until smooth and glossy.
10. Mix in the crushed digestive biscuits with the chocolate mixture until well coated.
11. Layer the chocolate-biscuit mixture evenly over the honeycomb pieces in the basket.
12. Place the basket into the air fryer and cook at 160°C for 20 minutes until the chocolate has set.
13. Allow the bars to cool completely before cutting and serving.

> **NUTRITION FACTS PER 100G:**
> Energy: 490 kcal | Protein: 4g | Total Fat: 24g | Saturated Fat: 14g
> Carbohydrates: 67g | Sugars: 58g | Dietary Fibre: 1g

Mini Banoffee Pies

SERVINGS: 6 MINI PIES | DIFFICULTY: EASY | TEMPERATURE: 180°C
PREPARATION TIME: 20 MINUTES | COOKING TIME: 10 MINUTES

Ingredients:

* 150g digestive biscuits
* 75g unsalted butter, melted
* 6 tbsp dulce de leche
* 2 ripe bananas, sliced
* 300ml double cream
* 2 tbsp icing sugar
* 1 tsp vanilla extract
* Grated chocolate or cocoa powder for garnish

Preparation:

1. Start by crushing the digestive biscuits into fine crumbs using a food processor or by placing them in a sealed bag and rolling over them with a rolling pin.
2. In a bowl, combine the biscuit crumbs with the melted butter and mix until well combined.
3. Firmly press the crumb mixture into the base and sides of 6 individual tartlet tins to form the pie crusts.
4. Preheat your air fryer to 180°C. Place the tartlet tins inside and cook for 5 minutes to set the crusts.
5. Remove the crusts from the air fryer and let them cool completely.
6. Spread one tablespoon of dulce de leche over each cooled crust.
7. Arrange the banana slices evenly on top of the dulce de leche layer.
8. Whip the double cream with the icing sugar and vanilla extract until soft peaks form.
9. Generously pipe or spoon the whipped cream onto the banana layer.
10. Finish by garnishing each mini pie with grated chocolate or a light dusting of cocoa powder.
11. Chill the mini pies in the fridge for at least 30 minutes before serving to set the layers.

NUTRITION FACTS PER 100G:
Energy: 334 kcal | Protein: 3g | Total Fat: 24g | Saturated Fat: 15g
Carbohydrates: 27g | Sugars: 19g | Dietary Fibre: 1g

Disclaimer

This book has been created with care to provide easy and delicious recipes for the Ninja Air Fryer and similar models. However, neither the author nor the publisher assumes any responsibility for potential damages that may result from the use of the recipes or instructions provided. Always follow the manufacturer's instructions for using your air fryer, as cooking times and temperatures may vary depending on the specific appliance and ingredients used.

Nutritional information provided in this book is based on average values and is meant for general guidance only. For specific dietary needs or health-related questions, please consult a nutritionist or healthcare professional.

The author and publisher make no guarantees regarding the accuracy or completeness of the information presented. Use of the content is at the reader's own risk.

EXCLUSIVE BONUS

40 Weight Loss Recipes

&

14 Days Meal Plan

Scan the QR-Code and receive
the FREE download:

Printed in Great Britain
by Amazon